D1737767

'In a culinary world full of froths, foams and smears, this is a book for those that love real food. It's a breath of fresh air and a feast for the eyes, full of mouth-watering recipes to excite the palate and take you to a gastronomic heaven.'

MICHEL ROUX JR

'Rosie Birkett is one of this country's most respected food writers and her enthusiasm and dedication to broaden her and her reader's horizons to the greater food spectrum is unquestionable. Full of passion, her fun and endearing personality is always reflected in the food and places that she writes about'

TOM KERRIDGE

'A beautiful and original book - contemporary, evocatively written and full of creative recipes you'll want to cook. Rosie is an exciting new voice in food.'

GIZZI ERSKINE

'For all the time I've known Rosie, she's always had 'a lot on her plate', and flicking through these pages, I sense a pace, energy and colour that reflects that. This is very much the food I imagined Rosie to bring to life in her book. Her recipes draw from lots of difference influences, cuisines, and styles, and yet manifest in a youthful, fresh, uncomplicated way.'

VIVEK SINGH

'Rosie is a good pal, great journalist and now an author... but above all a cracking cook!'

GLYNN PURNELL

PRAISE FOR

A lot on her plate

'Stuffed full of clever recipes I wish I'd written, and am desperate to try, this gorgeous, colourful book is as fun, and as lively as the very talented Rosie herself. I am very jealous.'

FELICITY CLOAKE, THE GUARDIAN + AUTHOR OF PERFECT

'Rosie's food is modern and clever yet comforting and familiar, and this recipe book is nothing short of brilliant.'

LULU GRIMES, OLIVE MAGAZINE

'This is a fabulous book, full of excellent recipes. Whatever the time of day or social event you will find something in here. Rosie's charm, wit and enthusiasm for all things food shine through in her writing.'

JAMES LOWE, LYLE'S

'*A Lot on Her Plate* by Rosie Birkett is a delightful read with truly beautiful photos. Rosie's story is candid and touching and her unapologetic "eat what you want" attitude is refreshing. This book will inspire you to visit your local suppliers and get creative in the kitchen. I love that she focuses on using the best ingredients to bring out the full potential of food and urges one to always cook from scratch. You will be inviting your friends over soon after reading this for the simple pleasure of enjoying one another's company over some delicious, honest home cooking.'

APRIL BLOOMFIELD

ROSIE BIRKETT

A lot on her plate

A new way to cook for two, a few or plenty

PHOTOGRAPHY BY **HELEN CATHCART**

CONTENTS

Foreword

When I first received the unedited proofs for *A Lot On Her Plate* I knew it would become a real cook's companion because I couldn't put it down. What I love about this book is the way Rosie has laid it out in a simple yet masterly way, something that only somebody who truly loves cooking and sharing can. To me, the hallmark of a great cook is a judicious eye with ingredients, treated simply and served with generosity, and that's what this book is all about.

I first met Rosie when she filled in for another journalist on maternity leave to go on one of our gastronomic trips to France. I remember it well: the working title for the trip was 'In search of the perfect Bouillabaise', and we were travelling to Marseille with one of the country's best maître d's and another Michelin-starred chef. When a slip of a girl with wild blonde hair and a huge holdall overflowing with girls' stuff turned up, we were skeptical because we needed a hardened food hack used to the rigours of a fast-paced trip, and up to meeting some of the world's greatest artisans and Michelin-starred chefs.

We shouldn't have worried, because after just five minutes in Rosie's company she bowled us over with her thirst for knowledge and genuine love of food. We saw that she was a girl after our own hearts, and we went on to eat some amazing food together, from a classic Bouillabaise simmered in a cast iron pot over an open fire, to a molecular Bouillabaise in a cocktail glass! Rosie completely got it, and after one special dinner we all sat together on Marsaille harbour wall with our feet dangling into the warm Med, whilst Rosie made her own contribution – a roll-up cigarette to smoke (she tells me she's since given up) while we relaxed and recalled our favourite dishes from the night.

Just a few hours later we were up at the crack of dawn visiting the vibrant fish market, located exactly where we'd been having our post-dinner puff, looking at the incredible day's catch – fish so fresh they were still gasping for air, and octopus making a run for it across the marble slabs. Anyone with a weak constitution would have turned green after having such a long dinner the night before, but not Rosie, all she could think about was where we were going to get breakfast!

Leafing through *A Lot on Her Plate* is a pleasure, and I am sure it will satisfy all level of cooks: from beginners trying a simple recipe like the Leeks vinaigrette; to everyday cooks, who can perfect the Mushroom ragout with truffled polenta; and more competent cooks, learning to master the Maple braised pigs cheeks.

Rosie has laid this book out in a way that encourages her readers to succeed. Care has been taken to explain how to shop wisely, which equipment to select, and what is required as mis en place before embarking on cutting, slicing, braising and searing. Most importantly to me, *A Lot on Her Plate* makes you want to get cooking!

Chris Galvin

CHRIS GALVIN

THE TITLE OF THIS BOOK, WHICH IS ALSO THE NAME OF MY BLOG, SAYS IT ALL REALLY.

It speaks of my love of a good meal – my tendency to literally fill my plate up given half a chance – but it also reveals a little about my life in general: the fact that like most young people trying to get on in today's economic climate, I'm usually balancing a few things at once, albeit while feeding my notably round face.

For me, cooking is about more than producing fuel for your body. It's one of life's simplest and most essential pleasures, and one of the fundamental things that makes us human. It underpins families, communities, cultures and histories, and brings people together in a way that nothing else can.

I've always thought that cooking is a little bit magical. You take something as simple and prosaic as a potato and transform it into something that makes you purr with pleasure: whether it's salted, vinegar-doused chips, golden, garlic-spiked roast spuds, or a creamy truffle-laced soup. These mouthfuls evoke emotional and sensory responses that are simultaneously universal and deeply personal. Cooking is remarkable in that sense, and it is absolutely one of the kindest, most creative things we can do for ourselves.

Aside from being relaxing and fun, cooking is also about looking after yourself and the ones you love, and being connected to the ingredients you're putting into your body is a good way of doing that. Anyone who knows me, knows I'm as partial to a toasted cheese sandwich or decadent restaurant meal as the next person – I'm a strong believer in eating what you want and balancing, rather than eschewing food groups (unless you have to) – and counting calories rather takes the pleasure out of things – but if you

cook from scratch you have more control over what you're consuming, and can make informed decisions about how you want to nourish yourself.

Cooking can also be one of life's greatest comforts. One of the toughest times in my life was the winter just after my father had died. I was 21, grieving and heartbroken, and still living in my student house in Leeds in the north of England. At a loss as to what I wanted to do, I was working in a miserable admin job that required me to travel to Grimsby on the coast of Lincolnshire throughout the week. This involved long, lonely waits on dark, freezing train platforms and far too much crying on public transport.

I would get in at about 8 pm, often to a deserted, dirty student kitchen. Cooking my evening meal was all I had to look forward to, and, after I'd cleared up the kitchen, I took great comfort in creating a warming, simple but satisfying meal for myself, usually while listening to music and drinking too much red wine. My repertoire then was limited, but whether it was a quick pasta dish or a fish pie, that meal reminded me of home, it reminded me of him, and it helped me get through a very difficult period in my life.

For me there is nothing on this earth I would rather do than bring together the people I love and share good food and wine with them. After all, conviviality is conducive to the best conversation and when we relax over a good meal, we free ourselves to marvel, plot and, importantly, laugh. We eat through joy and heartbreak, to celebrate and to grieve, alone and together.

We eat to live, but, when we can, there's nothing better than living to eat.

Where it all began

If I had to describe my definitive childhood food memory, it would be the image of my mother – her ash-blonde hair clipped back, a cigarette to hand (I know, I know, but it *was* the 80s) and a glass of cold white wine by her side – at the kitchen counter, seasoning a joint of beef for her legendary Sunday roast; washing still-muddy vegetables from our garden, whipping cream into soft clouds for pavlova or doing any other number of delectable things.

She was, and still is, my first inspiration when it comes to home cooking. She brought us up on well-made meals cooked from scratch that were always so tasty we would clamour for seconds. Stewed lamb with sweet pickled walnuts, buttery mounds of mashed potato and sweet peas from the garden; hunks of rare roast beef that we'd dredge through rich meaty gravy and slather in creamy horseradish, or scoff cold from the fridge clasped to a golden Yorkshire pudding – this was the food of my childhood.

My parents, who met as news journalists covering the IRA's siege of Balcombe Street in 1975, abandoned London to bring up me and my older, sister Alice, in the depths of the Kent countryside, and I wouldn't swap the memories I have of long garden lunches, early morning mushrooming, or summer evening barbecues for anything. Our kitchen was the first room you came into when you entered the house, and it always smelled rich and homely with the fragrance of Mum's cooking. It's a bit of a joke in my family that when I cuddled my mother as a little girl, I'd often say to her, 'You smell so good, just like stew.'

My father, Peter Birkett, was a Fleet Street journalist and news editor with a tremendous spirit and lust for life, and as big an appetite for food and wine as he had for a good story. As a young reporter living in Northern Ireland during the Troubles, he'd phone his copy through to the subs' desks without ever needing to write it down, and his strong head for news saw him work in senior positions at national newspapers, commuting to London daily to make sure we were provided for.

At home in Kent, he was 'foraging' way before it was cool. I remember him getting almost hysterical about the start of Kent's short cobnut season, when from about August to October, he'd declare war on squirrels; shooting at them out of the bedroom window with an air rifle, and obsessively raiding the cobnut trees with a plastic bag in his hand, later sitting at the kitchen table with a pair of nutcrackers and a large gin and tonic, shelling these gorgeously juicy, fresh crunchy nuts.

In those days I was more interested in cooking up inedible mud and nettle stews over a camp fire than spending time in the kitchen with my mother. But as years progressed, I became more and more interested in Mum's cooking: observing the way she browned meat before gently nestling it into her battered Le Creuset with softened onions, and admiring the thrifty way she'd eke out dripping from a never-ending bowl she kept in the fridge, saving up leftover stock or gravy, her freezer an Aladdin's cave of well-labelled Tupperware.

My mum put particular effort into evening and weekend meals because they were the precious times that we were all together, and they were the times that I really got to know my father. And I'm so pleased I did, because I lost him very suddenly when I was 21, a week before graduating from university. I had studied English, with a view to following in his footsteps and going into journalism. He had no idea that I would go on to forge a career centered on one of his biggest passions, but when I think about my dad, it makes me very happy to know that our relationship was always so bound-up in food.

What this book's about

During my time as a food writer, I've had the incredible fortune to observe, interview and sample the cooking of some of the world's best chefs: from Heston Blumenthal, René Redzepi, and April Bloomfield to Fergus Henderson and Alain Ducasse. Writing stories about food has taken me to some exotic, far-flung places and given me some delicious, and some downright bizarre, one-off experiences; from squatting on my haunches barbecuing lemongrass pork with Vietnamese women in Hanoi, to sharing a tub of buttery whelks with Pierre Koffmann and Alain Roux at a seafood café on the edge of Paris's Rungis market. Then there was that time I ate a mealworm muffin and a cricket samosa in a Dutch university in the name of 'research'. I've loved it all, and I truly believe that there's never been a more exciting time to be interested in food.

One of the biggest things I've learned by getting in the way of chefs in their kitchens, is that a great dish starts with the ingredients. But I don't just mean slabs of foie gras or fresh hauls of hand-dived scallops. I mean a bunch of peppery parsley, sprig of wild garlic or shin of beef. Most chefs I know are just as likely to get excited by humble produce – the first sweet green pea or the under-used cut of meat – as they are luxury ingredients. And while they're a varied, charmingly obsessive and unique bunch, if there's one thing they all agree on, it's finding the best-quality produce you can, from the best possible source.

The recipes in this book will help you to think a little bit more like a chef about the ingredients you're cooking with. They will, I hope, encourage you to explore your local markets and shops, butchers, delis and fishmongers, and investigate producer-direct box schemes for fresh well-sourced produce, and transform it into exciting, flavoursome, globally-influenced dishes for yourself and your loved ones. The book also offers ideas for making tasty, beautiful food on a tighter budget, using fridge, freezer and store-cupboard staples, and leftovers perked up with a couple of key fresh ingredients, so that you can cook wow-factor food, without breaking the bank.

I hope it will nudge you to try out some new ingredients, too – that cut of meat you weren't sure how to cook, or that piece of seafood you thought looked a bit daunting to prepare – and open up your repertoire to include recipes that you wouldn't have cooked before. I want to inspire you to get creative, be a bit more daring and leave yourself open to finding new ingredients, or use well-known ingredients in a new way.

HOW TO SHOP

This book is not about supermarket bashing. I know that many people, myself included, are short of time and money, and sometimes depend on the convenience and value provided by the supermarkets. But, taken as a single source for food shopping, I don't think they do much for our culinary imaginations, or for the food culture of our local areas.

When we only shop at the supermarket we are swamped by choice, and led by buy-one-get-one-free promotions and discount offers, rather than by the seasons. We are offered meat and fish pre-cut and packed in plastic, rather than being given information on which bits to cook and which to discard. We are isolated as we shop, rushing past each other with trolleys, talking into mobile phones as the self-checkout tells us to 'place the item in the bagging area'. Not exactly inspiring.

This way of shopping can make us complacent about the way we consume, sugar-coating us in a comfort zone where we buy cheaper, lower-quality ingredients in greater volumes than we need, cook repetitively and end up throwing much of our food away. Food waste is one of the biggest scandals of the modern age, and I think much of our throwaway attitude to ingredients can be linked to our disconnection to them.

I understand that not everyone has good access to markets or fishmongers, butchers, delis and greengrocers. Not everyone is self-employed or so obsessed with food that they want to spend free time hunting around for ingredients. And sourcing ingredients can be very time consuming, let's be honest. But if you've picked up this book then you are probably interested in cooking and in where ingredients come from, and I would encourage you to start shopping around a bit more, if you're not already, even if it's just on your days off or at weekends.

Think about how much meat you're consuming, too. I'm a huge fan of cooking and eating meat, but I'm also a firm believer that eating less, better-quality meat is kinder for our health and for our planet. It is now perfectly possible for food lovers to eat a largely plant-based diet and be sated. One of my favourite food writers Michael Pollan coined the mantra 'Eat food. Not too much. Mostly plants', and I'm inclined to agree with him. In the same vein, I buy organic wherever possible because I think the produce tastes better, doesn't contain any nasty chemicals, and is better for the universe and for our precious bees, who heroically pollinate some of our most prized foodstuffs – avocados, cherries and onions to name just a few.

GET TO KNOW YOUR LOCAL SUPPLIERS

If you don't live in an area served well by markets, there are some amazing producer-driven box schemes out there that can connect you directly to local farms and producers, as well as local growing initiatives that you can find by doing a little bit of research. If you spend just a bit more time thinking about sourcing you might just find, like I have, that it does wonders for your food, and for your wallet.

Fishmongers, greengrocers, markets and butchers – places where you can chat, shop, gossip, brainstorm recipes, learn about ingredients and generally get looked after – once formed the backbone of the food supply chain, but now they're a dying breed. Seek out your

local ones and look at what they've got to offer. Speak to them and try and get to know them. You'll soon figure out if these traders are any good and if they are sourcing their produce from trusted suppliers. If you live in a multicultural area, suss out different communities' shops too: they are often wonderlands of interesting, unusual and new ingredients and flavours, and can be hugely inspiring.

We've become so used to supermarket meat that we eat way too much of it, often consuming added salt and preservatives in the process. We're so disconnected from the blood, guts and death of slaughter, that we've started to complain that carcasses on display in butchers' windows are

offensive. With ignorance comes fear: fear of not knowing what to buy or who to speak to – fear of looking foolish.

I can't count the number of times I've felt a bit silly going into the butcher's shop and asking questions. But most of the time I have been greeted with informed, helpful answers, told about cuts of meat that save me money, given tips for how to cook them and gleaned assurance about where the meat has come from. I also know that when I'm in there, watching them chop through flesh or saw through bone, I am faced with the death of an animal, and I have the utmost respect for that meat I take home. I make a fuss of it when I cook it, and savour the eating of it.

We shouldn't view these specialists as unapproachable or intimidating. They are tradesmen and women who know their subject inside out and who are trying to make a living, and the good ones will strive to help you – be it with finding an ingredient, telling you what's in season or what's been grown/reared locally, how much of it you need and how to cook it. Crucially, they will work with your budget and help you find something that suits your needs, while informing you about their products. They have years of experience, knowledge and passion, and they are usually very happy to share it and any recipes they might have up their sleeves.

MAKE GREAT FOOD,
WHETHER YOU'RE FLUSH OR FRUGAL

To say that my life today is different to how I grew up is an understatement. Like many of my generation, making ends meet is harder than it was for my parents, and getting on the property ladder is just out of reach. I live in a rented, one bedroom basement flat in Hackney, East London, which I absolutely love, but which has the smallest kitchen – to use my father's favourite hyperbole – *known to man*. But having very limited kitchen space hasn't stopped me coming up with some cracking recipes, and it shouldn't stop anyone. After all, many of the world's greatest cuisines are cooked with modest means and facilities.

The recipes in this book reflect the 'flush or frugal' way I cook and eat. Some of them are super cheap to make (I'm looking at you, Baby potato and rosemary pizzas on page 97), while others, like Bavette steak with bottarga butter (see page 118), will need you to spend a bit more on them. If I'm having a lean month, which, being self-employed and a writer, happens a lot, I tend to cook economically, using up trusty bits from the store cupboard, fridge and freezer, perked up by cheaper fresh ingredients like bunches of herbs, avocado or my go-to cheap eat: eggs. I find that it's much better to shop as I go, rather than doing bulk shops, as this prevents me from wasting food and means that I often end up basing a recipe around one star fresh ingredient and other things I know I've got in the cupboard or fridge (hello, Smoked mackerel risotto on page 129).

Because I don't like to buy cheap meat if I can help it, I tend to go easy on the meat during these times, instead using up cured meats or bacon as a condiment to season or add a meaty twist. When I do cook with meat, I tend to choose cheaper cuts of well-reared, higher welfare, preferably British animals from my trusted butcher. As such, this book doesn't include any recipes for huge racks of lamb or prime joints of beef, but encourages you

to embrace lesser-used cuts that can be just as, if not more, tasty than their better-known cousins, when cooked to their full potential.

When I've been paid and am feeling a little more flush, I usually celebrate by stocking up on things I need (a well-stocked store cupboard is essential to creating great meals on a budget) and lovely fresh, seasonal ingredients – perhaps a nice piece of meat or seafood, or a specialist ingredient, like bottarga, that I know will go a long way and add some real 'wow' to dishes. When I buy expensive ingredients like truffle oil or nduja (the gorgeous soft and spicy Calabrian sausage), I want to be able to eke them out over a few dishes, or use them in smaller quantities in condiments, starters, salads or small plates to be savoured. I still cook strategically at times like these, so I might buy a nice corn-fed chicken and make some really good chicken stock that can be frozen and dipped into, or do a slow braise that will keep us going for a few days.

HANDY SHOPPING TIPS

> Make lists, shop as you go and use up what you have in: we waste way too much food by overstuffing our fridges. Allow yourself to be led by what ingredients you might find and by what's in season, and occasionally have a kitchen purge where you use up everything that's hanging around the fridge, freezer or cupboard. You'll save yourself some money and have fun stocking up again.
> Find out about your local farmers' market or farm shop, and start popping in at the weekend to stock up on their seasonal bounties.

MEAT AND POULTRY

> Look out for local or domestic meat with Red Tractor, Organic, Biodynamic or Free Range accreditation, or details of the farm it comes from, the breed and any information about the way it's been reared. Don't be afraid to ask your butcher for these details – they should be happy to share them.
> Cheaper and on-the-bone cuts like oxtail, lamb neck, shank, shin, cheeks, bavette and skirt steak will save you a small fortune and pack a massive flavour punch.

FISH AND SEAFOOD

> Check that fish and seafood have shiny rather than cloudy eyes and blood-red gills, and don't smell fishy – as a rule, fresh fish shouldn't smell strong.
> Look for fish and seafood that has been caught sustainably – keep an eye out for things like line- or pole-caught fish and 'hand dived' rather than 'trawled' scallops and clams.
> We all know by now that many fish stocks are endangered or on their way to being so. A helpful website is www.msc.org: it tells you which fish and seafood are plentiful and sustainable to eat now.

EQUIPMENT

You don't need specialist equipment to make the recipes in this book, though if you want to invest in one thing, I would recommend investing in a pasta machine if you don't already have one, and getting a cheap piping bag has really opened up my pastry repertoire. Most of my recipes can be made with the most rudimentary of kitchen kit, and I've certainly been known to improvise when a recipe has called for something that I don't happen to have (perversely, I once made Yorkshire puddings in a madeleine tray). Below are some of the things that I find very useful to have in my kitchen, starting off with what I'd say is absolutely essential, and gradually getting less so.

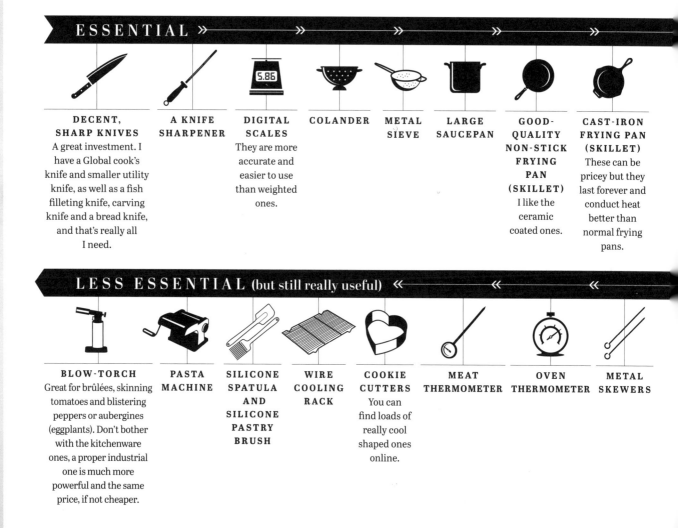

ESSENTIAL »

DECENT, SHARP KNIVES
A great investment. I have a Global cook's knife and smaller utility knife, as well as a fish filleting knife, carving knife and a bread knife, and that's really all I need.

A KNIFE SHARPENER

DIGITAL SCALES
They are more accurate and easier to use than weighted ones.

COLANDER

METAL SIEVE

LARGE SAUCEPAN

GOOD-QUALITY NON-STICK FRYING PAN (SKILLET)
I like the ceramic coated ones.

CAST-IRON FRYING PAN (SKILLET)
These can be pricey but they last forever and conduct heat better than normal frying pans.

LESS ESSENTIAL (but still really useful) «

BLOW-TORCH
Great for brûlées, skinning tomatoes and blistering peppers or aubergines (eggplants). Don't bother with the kitchenware ones, a proper industrial one is much more powerful and the same price, if not cheaper.

PASTA MACHINE

SILICONE SPATULA AND SILICONE PASTRY BRUSH

WIRE COOLING RACK

COOKIE CUTTERS
You can find loads of really cool shaped ones online.

MEAT THERMOMETER

OVEN THERMOMETER

METAL SKEWERS

ELECTRICAL EQUIPMENT

MINI CHOPPER

My Cuisinart one is one of the most-used things in my kitchen, for making dips, grinding spices, making dressings, salsas, curry pastes and sauces.

STICK BLENDER

Makes light work of soups and smoothies.

STAND MIXER

It was a watershed moment when I got my KitchenAid – it's like having a spare pair of hands in the kitchen.

FOOD PROCESSOR

So great to have for cutting down prep time, if you have the space.

SMALL DEEP-FAT FRYER

Fab for making proper chips and fritters.

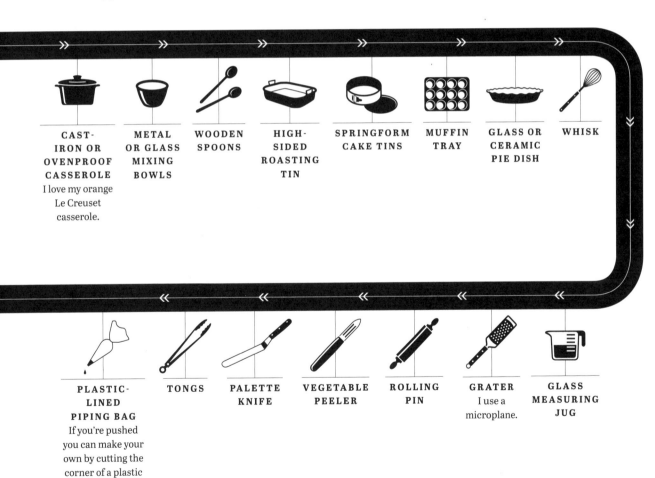

CAST-IRON OR OVENPROOF CASSEROLE

I love my orange Le Creuset casserole.

METAL OR GLASS MIXING BOWLS

WOODEN SPOONS

HIGH-SIDED ROASTING TIN

SPRINGFORM CAKE TINS

MUFFIN TRAY

GLASS OR CERAMIC PIE DISH

WHISK

PLASTIC-LINED PIPING BAG

If you're pushed you can make your own by cutting the corner of a plastic sandwich bag.

TONGS

PALETTE KNIFE

VEGETABLE PEELER

ROLLING PIN

GRATER

I use a microplane.

GLASS MEASURING JUG

BASIC INGREDIENTS

Here are some ingredients I like to try and have in stock: I find this lot keeps me very well equipped to make my favourite recipes and throw something delicious together in a hurry.

If you have a front step, windowsill or any outdoor space, no matter how humble, I'd really encourage you to grow your own herbs. It's so cheap and easy to do, and there's something wonderfully smug about being able to pick, rather than buy, your own fresh, food-mile-free food. I grow parsley, sage, thyme, rosemary and bay, and they're the gift that keep on giving, demanding nothing more than a regular watering!

I buy organic milk, butter and eggs because they taste better and are better for the planet. I only ever buy unsalted butter, so when I list butter in the recipes, I mean unsalted. If I want salted butter, I just scatter it with crunchy flakes of Maldon sea salt. On that note, I prefer to use Maldon for pretty much everything apart from salting water for vegetables and pasta. I just love the crystals!

STORE-CUPBOARD

Baking powder

Basmati rice

Capers: little buds of juicy, salty joy, which spruce up any fish dish or dressing.

Coconut milk and desiccated coconut

Dried mushrooms

Fast-action dried yeast

Flours: organic plain white flour, rye flour, buckwheat flour (great for making quick galettes for breakfast: just mix with water, salt and pepper, and 1 egg to make a batter, and fry like pancakes in a really hot pan), cornflour (cornstarch).

Fried red onion: I get this in tubs from the Vietnamese supermarket – great for adding crunch to poached eggs or avocado on toast.

Fruit: tinned lychees, tinned black cherries, maraschino cherries, golden sultanas.

Grilled red peppers: in vinegar.

Herbs & spices: ground cumin and cumin seeds, coriander seeds, fennel seeds, black peppercorns, ground white pepper, cayenne pepper, garam masala, dried chilli flakes, dried chipotle chillies, star anise, nutmeg, garlic granules, dried tarragon.

Kalamata olives

Lentils: dried puy or small green lentils (cooked with bay leaves and black peppercorns they make for a frugal and filling lunch, or are great for eating with roasted meats like the porchetta on page 154).

Nuts: ground almonds, toasted flaked almonds (brilliant for impromptu desserts), hazelnuts (I've always got a packet on the go, for snacking, throwing into granola or toasting and adding a nutty crunch to pasta dishes, crumbles or salads).

Oils: invest in a good-quality extra-virgin olive oil (for salad dressings, finishing dishes and having with bread), light olive oil, truffle oil, rapeseed oil, coconut oil, vegetable oil, groundnut oil.

Pasta: spaghetti, orecchiette and other dried pastas (when my fridge is bare I use dried pasta for simple suppers, sometimes just with a crushed fresh garlic clove, olive oil, salt and pepper, a sprinkling of chilli flakes and Parmesan).

Peanut butter: (I love to spread it onto a crusty baguette and top with an omelette, some coriander and Sriracha for a makeshift *bánh mì*).

Pomegranate molasses

Quinoa: a great way to bulk-up salads or create an impromptu lunch. Cook with a stock cube or bay leaves to give it a bit more flavour. Experiment with different colours.

Rice noodles

Sauces: light soy sauce, good fish sauce, Sriracha, Worcestershire sauce and Tabasco.

Sea salt

Seeds: chia seeds, pumpkin seeds, sunflower seeds, sesame seeds (black and white).

Shrimp paste

Sugars: muscovado sugar, caster (superfine) sugar (I like golden), icing (confectioners') sugar.

Tahini

Tinned beans & pulses: cannellini beans (blitz up with garlic and olive oil for a simple dip, use as the base for a stew, cassoulet or salad, or just eat them rinsed, drizzled with olive oil and seasoned with salt, pepper and some parsley), chickpeas (great for whizzing up with tahini, lemon juice and garlic for a quick hummus), black beans (the perfect partner to Mexican food, see page 93).

Tinned fish: anchovies (I can't live without these fishy little fiends – track down the salt-packed ones if you can, because they have a very special flavour, but regular anchovies in tins and jars do wonders for any salad, sauce, slow braise or dip), mackerel (fillets like the tinned mackerel in oil are great on toasted sourdough for a quick lunch), sardines, soft cod's roe, smoked oysters or mussels (great for adding umami or whipping up canapés), tuna fillets in olive oil.

Tinned tomatoes: I find whole plum tomatoes have a better flavour.

Vinegars: red wine vinegar, white wine vinegar, sherry vinegar, cider vinegar (I like the unpasteurised kind with mother), rice wine vinegar and tarragon vinegar.

Wakame (dried seaweed)

FRESH

Avocados: smash onto toast with salt, a squeeze of lime and chilli flakes for a meal in itself.

Corn tortillas: from Mexican stores.

Dripping: reserve from the roasting tin.

Eggs: a meal in a shell. Organic and free-range, if you please. I use medium in this book (unless otherwise stated).

Fresh ginger: so good for restorative teas, adding to smoothies, stir-fries and curries.

Garlic: the fresher the better, don't let it get all dry and crusty (old garlic is very overpowering). Cut out the green shoots!

Lemons: unwaxed

Limes

Wheat tortillas

Yoghurt: live probiotic – Greek is best. I prefer full-fat versions for adding body and sourness to sauces, salads, dressings and marinades.

FRIDGE

Baby gem lettuce: a good trick is to separate the leaves, wash them, bag them up and keep them in the crisper – they'll last longer.

Birdseye chilli

Carrots

Celery: it keeps for ages and is always handy when making braises, stocks, stews or sauces.

Courgettes (zucchinis)

Fresh herbs: basil, mint, coriander (cilantro) and parsley. Parsley is your best friend. It's healthy, cheap, readily available from corner shops and easily livens up any dish when whizzed into a simple salsa verde or dressed in a perky mustard vinaigrette.

Kale: keeps for ages and adds a bit of green goodness to any salad, soup or stew.

Leeks

Mayonnaise

Milk: organic is best.

Miso: great for adding umami to marinades.

Mustard: Dijon, wholegrain and English.

Onions

Parmesan

Preserved lemons

Spring onions (scallions)

Tomato purée

Unsalted butter

FREEZER

Blueberries

Broad (fava) beans

Chicken stock

Curry leaves

Ice

Pasta dough

Pastry

Peas

Peeled, chopped bananas: great for instant smoothies.

Pitta bread

Pizza dough

Sliced sourdough: slice a loaf of sourdough then freeze.

The recipes in this book have been tested using a fan-assisted oven. If you have a conventional oven, increase the heat by 20°C. Ovens vary in temperature so invest in an oven thermometer to check yours.

I'm not one of those 'I'LL SKIP DESSERT' types.

CHAPTER 1

Breakfast +brunch

I LOVE BREAKFAST.

I'm not someone who can skip it, but then, why would you want to? It's the first chance in the day to eat, and while I appreciate that not everyone has the freelancer's blessing of being able to cook first thing in the morning, I think giving yourself a delicious start to the day is important. It also makes getting out of bed that little bit less painful. I hope the recipes in this chapter will inspire you to try out some new flavours and breakfast dishes, and leave that packet of shop-bought cereal in the cupboard for when you come home drunk and hungry.

My recipe for Coconut and almond granola, on page 31, which is low in sugar and great with either almond milk or coconut water, is a quick and fabulous alternative to milk-drenched cereal. You can make a big batch of it at the weekend – it will fill your house with a gorgeous toasty aroma – and then work your way through it during the week. On weekends I love nothing more than getting the newspaper and making a cooked brunch with my boyfriend Jamie: it's nice to be able to sit down together for the first meal of the day, as we so rarely do during the busy working week.

This chapter is very globally inflected, because while England obviously own the Full English (and my favourite, Marmite on toast), I think there's a huge amount we can learn from other countries' breakfasting habits. I've been massively influenced by the breakfasts I've eaten all over the world, on my travels, and these recipes reflect

my wanderlust. In Australia, during my university vacation, I was blown away by the emphasis they put on breakfasts in their cafés and restaurants, and savoured the fresh fruit smoothies, plates of gorgeous Eggs Benedict and deep bowls of smooth, creamy coffee.

On my first visit to New York, I remember the ecstasy of sitting at the polished counter of an old-fashioned diner near Madison Avenue, eating a plate of fluffy pancakes with a slick of glistening maple syrup and the crunchiest bacon I'd ever had. Vietnamese breakfasts were all about the addictively sweet iced coffees, thick with condensed milk, slathering Laughing Cow 'cheese' onto airy *bánh mì* baguettes and gobbling bags of pineapple and melon dipped in chilli and lime salt. In Mumbai, while reporting on the crumbling Parsi cafés throughout the city, I drank enough chai to flood the Taj Mahal, and feasted on turmeric-spiced, coriander-flecked eggs and freshly baked *pau* – Portuguese bread rolls.

But it was Mexico, with its ever-inventive breakfasts of corn tortillas, onion, different chilli salsas, eggs cooked in various guises, and fresh ripe avocado, that stole my breakfasting heart. Any nation that eats avocado at breakfast as a matter of course gets my endorsement, and being a huge sucker for eggs and chilli at breakfast time (an amazing combination for kick-starting your metabolism), I just can't get enough. I hope you feel the same way about these recipes.

Cod's roe + sweetcorn fritters with avocado + Sriracha

W hen we were kids, a long, long time before it became the trendy 'dude food' it is today, my mum would occasionally make 'chicken Maryland' – her version of southern fried chicken. My favourite part of the dish was the sweetcorn fritters. I just loved the way the sweet, crunchy corn burst in my mouth, cloaked in savoury, spicy pancake batter. The addition of soft cod's roe to these fritters gives them a lovely light, fluffy texture and subtle fish flavour. I like these for brunch, but you can make a batch, fry them and freeze them. They're great reheated in the oven as a snack when entertaining friends, or when you just fancy something a bit naughty to nibble on. Dipped in spicy Sriracha chilli sauce, they are dangerously addictive!

600–800 ml (20–30 fl oz) flavourless oil (groundnut or sunflower), for deep-frying

100 g (3½ oz/½ cup) tinned, drained cod's roe, patted dry with kitchen paper

100 g (3½ oz/½ cup) tinned, drained sweetcorn

juice of ½ lemon

½ teaspoon ground white pepper

pinch of cayenne pepper

freshly ground black pepper

½ teaspoon sea salt

80 g (3 oz/⅔ cup) plain (all-purpose) flour

pinch of caster (superfine) sugar

grated zest of 1 lime

1 teaspoon southern spice mix or ¼ teaspoon each of hot smoked paprika, cayenne pepper, ground cumin and garlic granules

½ teaspoon baking powder

1 egg, beaten

60 ml (2 fl oz) milk

TO SERVE

Sriracha sauce or Sriracha mayo (see page 241)

1 ripe avocado, stoned and sliced

red chilli flakes, for sprinkling

wedges of lime, for squeezing

> Heat the oil in a deep-fat fryer or fill a large, high-sided pan with 3 cm (1½ in) oil. The oil should reach 185°C/365°F (test with a jam thermometer if using a pan).

> In a large bowl, gently mix the cod's roe with the sweetcorn, trying not to mash up the roe too much. Add the lemon juice and season generously with white pepper, cayenne pepper and black pepper. In a separate bowl, mix the salt, flour, sugar, lime zest, spices and baking powder. In a jug, mix the egg and milk with 1 tablespoon of cold water, and then whisk this into the flour mix until you have a loose-ish batter, just a fraction thicker than pancake batter, adding a touch more water if it's too thick.

> Add enough batter to the cod's roe and sweetcorn mix to coat them well so that they will hold together when fried. There may be some batter leftover, which you can keep in the fridge for a couple of days. Working in batches, carefully drop dessertspoonfuls of the mixture into the hot oil, 2 or 3 at a time, depending on the size of your fryer or pan. Leave them to cook, untouched, for about 4 minutes per batch, until they are a deep golden colour and have floated to the surface. Remove them carefully with a slotted spoon to a metal plate or baking tray covered with kitchen paper to absorb any excess fat. Scatter with salt and keep them warm in the oven on a low heat while you repeat the process with the remaining batter.

> Serve warm, with Sriracha sauce or Sriracha mayo, avocado and sprinkled with red chilli flakes and lime juice.

Coconut + almond granola

I tend to avoid cereal. It just doesn't do it for me. But one exception has to be home-made granola. Not only is it super easy to make, but it has a lovely, satisfying crunchy texture and is a great vehicle for goodness in the form of nuts and seeds. If you take the time to make a big batch once in a while, you'll find that you always have some in the cupboard for those days when you want a quick and easy, light yet filling breakfast. This recipe combines two of my favourite ingredients – almonds and coconut – and is divine eaten with coconut water or almond milk instead of cow's milk, though it's good with cow's milk too.

350 g (12 oz/3½ cups) organic jumbo oats

1 teaspoon chia seeds (available from most health-food stores)

80 g (3 oz) pumpkin seeds

15 g (½ oz) sunflower seeds

150 g (5 oz/1⅔ cups) flaked almonds

50 g (2 oz/½ cup) desiccated coconut

1½ teaspoons mixed sweet ground spices such as ground cinnamon, ginger and nutmeg

4 tablespoons coconut oil (available from most health-food stores), melted

4 tablespoons maple syrup

60 g (2 oz/½ cup) sultanas

❯ Preheat the oven to 180°C (350°F/Gas 4). Line a baking or roasting tray with baking paper.

❯ Put the oats, seeds, almonds, coconut and spices in a large mixing bowl. Pour over the melted coconut oil and maple syrup, and stir or mix with your hands until the oil and syrup are well incorporated. Spread the mixture out on the roasting tray in an even layer and bake for 15–20 minutes, stirring occasionally, until the oats and almonds take on a deep golden colour and crisp up. Remove from the oven and leave to cool for a few minutes before adding the sultanas. Leave to cool completely then store in a sealed container for up to 1 month.

Elly's pea, feta + spring onion frittata

My pal Elly Curshan makes the best frittatas. She runs the gorgeous Pear Café in Bristol, and we became friends on Instagram before we actually met, thanks to Elly's delicious pictures of her food. She's famous for her daily changing frittatas, and was kind enough to give me a favourite recipe from her repertoire. Pea, spring onion (scallion) and feta work really well together, but you can use the base recipe and customise it as you like, playing around with other ingredients. Check Elly's Instagram (@ellypear) for inspiration!

10 medium
new potatoes

1 tablespoon butter

1 tablespoon olive oil

6 eggs

sea salt and freshly
ground black pepper

6 tablespoons
grated Cheddar

155 g (5 oz/1 cup)
garden peas, cooked

3 spring onions
(scallions), finely sliced

70 g (2¼ oz) feta,
crumbled

> Boil the potatoes in salted water for 10–15 minutes until tender. Drain, cool and slice into 1 cm (½ in) discs. Heat the butter and oil in a large (25 cm/10 in) non-stick frying pan (skillet) over a medium heat and fry the potatoes until golden brown on both sides.

> Turn your grill on to its highest setting. Break the eggs into a large jug and whisk well, adding 3 tablespoons of water along with a large pinch of sea salt and a good few turns of black pepper. Whisk well and stir in the Cheddar. Add the fried potatoes, peas and spring onions to the jug and stir well, then pour the mix into the frying pan. Sprinkle over the feta and grill until golden on top and set to your liking (I prefer mine still a little bit wobbly in the middle). Set to one side for about 5 minutes, then slice and serve.

Super green kale smoothie

We all have days when we wake up feeling a bit jaded, regretful about that final 'small glass' from the night before, or just plain 'meh, it's Monday'. Working in food involves eating out a fair bit, so I've been known to harbour the odd 'food hangover'. When I was living in Vancouver I got into kale smoothies, because they were everywhere. They make me feel better. Kale is packed full of good things, from antioxidants and calcium, to vitamin C and beta carotene, and is a great way to give yourself a morning boost, which, not being a morning person at all, I desperately need. If you can't find coconut water (also a brilliant source of good things like potassium and minerals), use pineapple or orange juice instead.

100 g (3½ oz) kale, washed, stems removed and leaves patted dry

thumb-sized piece of fresh ginger, peeled and grated

1 ripe banana, peeled

600 ml (20 fl oz) coconut water

2 teaspoons runny honey

squeeze of lemon juice

SPECIAL EQUIPMENT

blender or food processor

> Put the kale, ginger and banana in a blender or food processor and blend to a pulp, then add the coconut water, honey and lemon juice. Blend thoroughly and drink straight away.

I'm not a morning person AT ALL, so I like a chilli-kick at breakfast.

Guacamole bread with fried eggs + chipotle salsa

T his recipe uses one of my all-time favourites – guacamole baked into a sort of cornbread. I say 'sort of' because I know how puritanical real US southerners get about cornbread, and I will leave the authentic stuff to them. But this is a lighter, greener version, made with polenta (because cornmeal is still infuriatingly hard to find in the UK), flavoured with herbs and spices, and given a moistness from the avocado and tomato. It's a good one to make if you've got friends coming for brunch, and is great served with fried eggs and smoky chipotle salsa.

120 g (4 oz/scant cup) polenta

1 teaspoon sea salt

1 teaspoon muscovado sugar

½ teaspoon baking powder

pinch of cayenne pepper

pinch of ground cumin

¼ teaspoon red chilli flakes

pinch of hot smoked paprika

4 tablespoons olive oil, plus extra for greasing

large handful of coriander (cilantro) leaves

1 garlic clove, peeled

30 g (1 oz) butter, melted and cooled

100 ml (3½ fl oz) whole milk

juice of 1 lime

1 egg, beaten

2 large, very ripe avocadoes, stoned, 1 cut into small cubes, 1 sliced

1 red onion, ½ diced, ½ sliced

1 large tomato, diced

TO SERVE

4–6 eggs

Chipotle salsa (see page 242)

‣ Preheat the oven to 220°C (425°F/Gas 7). Grease a high-sided ovenproof dish, ovenproof frying pan (skillet) or high-sided baking tray and pop it in the oven until it's stinking hot.

‣ Place the polenta, salt, sugar, baking powder, spices, chilli flakes and paprika in a bowl and mix to combine.

‣ Make a herb oil by whizzing the oil with the coriander and garlic in a mini-chopper or pounding together in a pestle and mortar.

‣ In a separate bowl, whisk together the melted butter, milk, herb oil, lime juice and egg. Pour the liquid ingredients into the polenta mixture and stir. Fold through the cubed avocado, diced red onion and tomato. Check the consistency of the mix and add a little water if you need to: you want quite a wet mix. Remove the hot dish from the oven and pour the mixture in, topping it with the sliced avocado and sliced red onion. Turn the oven temperature down to 200°C (400°F/Gas 6) and bake for 20–25 minutes, checking it's not burning (cover the dish with foil if it is beginning to burn), until puffed and golden. Remove from the oven and leave to cool.

‣ Fry 4–6 eggs and serve with the bread and Chipotle salsa on the side.

Kale + coriander pancakes with slow-roasted tomatoes + avocado cream

This is my healthier version of the cherished breakfast pancake – stuffed full of goodness in the form of kale and coriander, with the slow-roasted tomatoes lending richness and acidity. But just because it's nourishing doesn't mean it has to be joyless, and the creamy, perky avocado cream made with tahini is sumptuous as hell. Make too much and then smear it on hot toasted sourdough. Or just eat it with your fingers like I do.

SLOW-ROASTED TOMATOES

2 large tomatoes, sliced into rounds, or 8 cherry tomatoes, halved

olive oil, for greasing and drizzling

sea salt and freshly ground black pepper

3 sprigs fresh thyme, leaves picked

KALE PANCAKES

100 g (3½ oz/scant cup) organic plain white (all-purpose) flour

½ teaspoon baking powder

grated zest of 1 lime

1 teaspoon garlic granules

1 teaspoon ground cumin

1 teaspoon sea salt

freshly ground black pepper

2 large kale leaves, washed and stems removed

35 g (1¼ oz) coriander (cilantro) leaves and stalks

100 ml (3½ fl oz) milk

1 egg, beaten

1 tablespoon olive oil

rapeseed oil, for frying

TO SERVE

Avocado cream (see page 81)

› Start by making the slow-roasted tomatoes. Preheat the oven to 160°C (320°F/ Gas 3). Place the tomato slices or halves on a greased baking tray or enamel plate, then drizzle with olive oil, season with salt and pepper, and scatter over the thyme leaves. Roast for 25–30 minutes, until they have softened and slightly shrivelled.

› While the tomatoes are roasting, make the pancake batter. Put the flour, baking powder, lime zest, spices, and salt and pepper into a mixing bowl. Blitz the kale leaves and coriander in a food processor until very finely chopped. Combine the milk, egg, olive oil, chopped kale and coriander in another bowl or jug. Pour the liquid ingredients into the flour mixture and whisk with a fork or balloon whisk, adding 1 tablespoon of cold water to the batter to loosen it, if necessary – you want it about the consistency of double (heavy) cream. Leave to rest while you make the avocado cream, and remove the tomatoes from the oven.

› To make the pancakes, dig out your best medium-sized non-stick frying pan (skillet) and a silicone brush or spatula. Pour about 1 tablespoon of rapeseed oil onto a small plate and brush your pan with the oil. Heat the pan over a high heat until stinking hot, then spoon about half a ladleful of the pancake mixture into the pan. Swirl the pan in a circular motion to evenly distribute the mixture – you're aiming for small, thick, American-style pancakes. Cook for 2–3 minutes and then shake the pan. When the pancake comes away from the bottom easily, flip it over and cook on the other side for 2 minutes, until golden. Transfer to a plate and cover with foil to keep warm. Repeat the process with the rest of the pancake mixture.

› Divide the pancakes between two plates and serve topped with the slow-roasted tomatoes and avocado cream.

Becky's migitas

When we were in Mexico, we were lucky enough to stay with our Mexican friend Becky, who is a brilliant home cook. The night we arrived in the sweltering heat of Playa Del Carmen, she helped us acclimatise with the most delicious fiery-hot enchiladas and freezer-chilled tequila. I've always been partial to a huevos rancheros, but Becky introduced me to this alternative egg dish of 'migitas' or 'migas' – fried corn tortilla, egg and onion hash best served with avocado and a hot salsa. Make sure you fry the corn tortillas until they're nice and crispy! I like to use both plain and blue tortillas for colour: you can get corn tortillas online or from Mexican grocers.

3 large eggs

pinch of sea salt

pinch of ground cumin

1 tablespoon milk

vegetable or groundnut oil, for frying

3 corn tortillas, cut into squares, triangles or strips

knob of butter

1 small white onion, finely sliced

1 green jalepeño chilli, deseeded and finely sliced

1 red jalepeño chilli, deseeded and finely sliced

TO SERVE

1 tablespoon chopped coriander (cilantro) leaves

Chipotle salsa (see page 242)

1 ripe avocado, stoned and sliced

lime wedges

> Lightly beat the eggs in a jug with the salt, cumin and milk. Set aside.

> Heat a tablespoon of oil in a heavy-based frying pan (skillet) and fry the tortilla slices until they're crispy all over. Transfer to a plate covered with kitchen paper to drain, and sprinkle them lightly with salt. Add a knob of butter to the pan and fry the onion and chilli until soft and the onion is starting to colour. Pour in the seasoned beaten eggs, followed by the crispy tortillas, and cook for a couple of minutes, until the eggs are just cooked but still fluffy and moist. Divide the *migitas* between two plates, garnish with fresh coriander and serve with the Chipotle salsa, avocado and lime.

41

Dishoom's akuri

You'll know by now that I've got a bit of a thing for eggs. Eggs are versatile, frugal, healthy and properly nourishing, and they really set you up for the day ahead. When I was in Bombay with the guys from London's Dishoom restaurant, visiting the city's Parsi cafés, I ate eggs in an entirely new way, fashioned into spicy omelettes, fries or scrambles with chillies, spices and onion. I noticed that many of the fading cafés and bakeries had old black-and-white photographs of body builders, and it was explained that the Iranis have a rich culture of body building, hence the penchant for eggs (many cafés dedicate whole sections on their menus to them). I gleaned this Parsi scrambled eggs recipe from Naved Nasir, Dishoom's executive chef. It's rich with restorative, medicinal turmeric (full with the antioxidant compound curcumin), and with chilli and coriander it's the ideal breakfast for someone in need of perking up.

---

25 g (1 oz) butter

1 small red onion, finely chopped

2 small tomatoes or 1 large tomato, finely chopped

pinch of chopped fresh green chilli

pinch of salt

pinch of red chilli powder (*deggi mirch*)

pinch of ground turmeric

4 eggs, lightly beaten

small handful of coriander (cilantro) leaves, finely chopped

TO SERVE

4 slices of toasted sourdough

grilled back bacon (optional)

2 stems of cherry tomatoes on the vine (optional)

❯ Put a heavy-based non-stick frying pan (skillet) over a high heat. Add the butter, onion, tomato, green chilli, salt, chilli powder and turmeric. Mix it all together and stir for 30 seconds, then let it sizzle for a few moments. Add 1 teaspoon of water.

❯ Add the eggs to the pan along with the chopped coriander. Stir the mixture for 30 seconds, then remove from the heat. The eggs should be soft and silky, rather than dry.

❯ Spoon the egg mixture over the sourdough toast, and serve with bacon and vine tomatoes on the side, if you wish.

Cumin brioche hangover-busting breakfast bap

This is my pimped-up version of the classic egg and bacon bap. As well-intentioned as the kale smoothie (see page 33) is, we all know that when you're really hanging, something much more evil, salty and greasy is needed to hit the spot. I came up with this little breakfast one morning after a launch party, when I had leftover Cumin brioche (see page 245) that needed using up. The lightly spiced demi-brioche is the perfect vehicle for thick bacon, a fried egg and some Sriracha chilli sauce – and we all know how much I love avocado, so I'd put some of that in there too. Any old bap will do, though the Cumin brioche does elevate it to a 'wow' dish.

4 thick slices of smoked back bacon

2 Cumin brioche (see page 245)

butter, for spreading

2 eggs

1 ripe avocado, stoned and sliced

Sriracha chilli sauce (optional)

> Turn on your grill and grill the bacon until it's cooked through and the fat is crisp (unless you don't like crispy bacon). Slice the brioche in half and toast them. Butter while hot. Fry the eggs then arrange the bacon on the bottom of the brioche, topped with an egg, slices of avocado and chilli sauce (if you wish). Enjoy.

Basted eggs with kale, lemon + chilli

I first had basted eggs in Oregon, where – being a proper egg geek – I was intrigued to learn about this cooking method which is a cross between poaching and frying. This is such a quick and simple recipe, it's something I usually turn to when there's not much food in the house, but I fancy a substantial but not too sinful start to the day. In this recipe the kale is steamed lightly when the eggs are almost done, then tossed in some lemon juice and chilli and eaten with the soft-yolky eggs and some toasted sourdough.

2 thick slices of sourdough bread

rapeseed or vegetable oil, for greasing

2 eggs

small knob of butter

50 g (2 oz) kale, washed and stems removed

½ lemon, for squeezing

extra-virgin olive oil, for dressing

pinch of red chilli flakes

salt and freshly ground black pepper

➤ The eggs cook really quickly, so it's best to put your toast on first. Grease a non-stick frying pan (skillet) with a little bit of oil, and set over a medium–high heat. When it's hot, crack in the eggs, and then add the butter and about 2 tablespoons of water. Cover with a lid or a plate and leave to cook for 1 minute. Add the kale leaves, cover and cook for another minute or two. Turn off the heat and remove the kale from the pan, toss in a little lemon juice, olive oil and chilli, and divide between plates with the eggs and toast. Season with salt and pepper and serve straight away.

CHAPTER 2

Starters + small plates

MY LOVE OF FISH AND SEAFOOD, WHICH FEATURES HEAVILY IN THIS CHAPTER OF SMALLER DISHES, UNQUESTIONABLY HARKS BACK TO CHILDHOOD, AND THE WARM, FUZZY MEMORIES I HAVE OF CAMPING HOLIDAYS IN FRANCE.

Forget trailer tents or practical, user-friendly caravans: when the Birketts hit Europe, we did so with our Conway 'Tardis', a miraculous but eccentric towable fold-up caravan that no other campers ever seemed to have heard of or seen before.

In Brittany, where we returned year after year, following the laborious rigmarole of building and unpacking the 'Tardis', my parents would bolt to the nearest beach restaurant and spend hours over *fruits de mer* platters with bottles of cold white wine. My sister and I invariably wolfed our *steak hachés* and *frites*, and scuttled off to the beach. After lunch we'd take long walks when the tide was out, filling buckets with cockles we'd later steam open and eat with white pepper and vinegar back at camp. My parents always planned to retire to France, and, if my father hadn't become very ill – for which years of treatment kept them in England – I believe that's what they would have done.

Because of his demanding job, time with my dad was precious growing up, and I would snatch any moments I could with him, whether it was – at his suggestion – him timing me as I ran around the garden while he drank gin and tonics (nice one, Dad), or building Meccano with him out of his old rusty toolbox. We had a shallow river running through the bottom of the garden where some trout lived, and spending a few quiet, reflective hours down there in the dappled sunlight with my dad playing at fishing is something I'll never forget.

A man of large appetites – for life, love, food and wine – it was he who introduced

me to the nutty, creamy delights of crab. For a treat, or to celebrate a 'good show' of his articles in the paper, he would buy a big live brown crab from the fishmonger, boil and dress it himself; clearing our kitchen table, spreading it with yesterday's newspaper, pouring himself a large drink, and mining the shell obsessively, a cigarette in the corner of his mouth and Radio 4 news blasting in the background. I would sit beside him, marvelling at the fearless way he cracked the claws with a hammer, and occasionally swiping bits of crab, much to his irritation. When he'd extracted all of the creature's meat, he'd gently mix it with a touch of mayonnaise, lemon juice and cayenne pepper, and then serve it to us to eat on good toast with sliced spring onion (scallions) and freshly ground black pepper.

There are a couple of crab recipes in this chapter, as well as some recipes that have been gleaned from my travels, like Mexican ceviche (see page 81), Crispy tuna tacos (see page 52) and Dishoom's Keema pau (see page 63). Like most cooks, I love discovering new foods and dishes, and travelling is always a huge source of inspiration, and something I try and take the opportunity to do when I can. If I find a new dish or flavour that I really love, I'll usually photograph it and try and figure out the recipe, either by talking to the chef or just by experimenting. Sometimes it's just a question of taking flavours that you like and having a play.

I hope you enjoy these dishes, which are designed to be shared, and work as starters or light meals in their own right. Of course, there's no reason why you couldn't up the quantities and make them into the main event if you're feeling greedy...

Smoked trout with griddled lemon, cucumber + sourdough croutons

This dish, Scandinavian in tone thanks to the pickles and smoked fish, takes ingredients that you may have lying around – lemon, cucumber and bread – and transforms them into something special, by charring them to add a smoky dimension and intensify their natural flavours. I get my smoked trout from Mike Scott, the chef at Hackney's wonderful Raw Duck restaurant, who smokes it himself at home, but this would work with any good-quality smoked fish, be it trout, mackerel or hot-smoked salmon.

1 tablespoon caster (superfine) sugar

1 tablespoon cider vinegar (get the good unpasteurised stuff if you can)

2 radishes, finely sliced

sea salt

2 baby or Lebanese cucumbers, cut in half lengthwise and halved across the middle

1 lemon, cut in half

1 slice of sourdough bread

6 tablespoons olive oil, plus extra for grilling

2 tablespoons roughly chopped dill

2 smoked trout fillets, skin removed

borage flowers, to garnish (optional)

4 teaspoons plain natural yoghurt, to serve

> Dissolve the sugar in the vinegar in a small bowl and quick-pickle the radish slices in the mixture.

> Heat a griddle pan over a high heat until it's stinking hot. Scatter with a pinch of sea salt. Brush the cucumber pieces, cut sides of the lemon and sourdough bread with olive oil and griddle for about 8 minutes, until there are black grill marks on them, turning the bread and cucumber over once.

> When the ingredients are grilled, remove from the heat and squeeze the lemon juice into a bowl with the olive oil. Whisk with a fork, add the dill and a pinch of salt, and whisk some more, until well combined. Cut the sourdough into croutons.

> Drain the radishes from their pickle liquor and place on kitchen paper to absorb the excess vinegar. Divide the cucumber between two plates and flake over the smoked trout. Top with the radish slices and drizzle over the dill and lemon oil. Scatter over the sourdough croutons and borage flowers, if using, and finish each serving with a couple of teaspoons of natural yoghurt.

Crispy sesame-crusted tuna tacos with mango salsa

When I lived in Vancouver, there was a wonderful Baja-inspired taco truck and commissary called *Tacofino that was famous for serving exciting, inventive tacos, and a fantastic array of tequilas. We had great nights there, and I always ordered the seared tuna tacos, which inspired this recipe. It fuses Asian and Mexican flavours, balancing sweet, sour, salty and spicy, and the mango salsa gives it a tropical edge. Try to track down corn tortillas as they really make the dish and add a satisfying crispy texture: you'll find them at Mexican grocers, delis or online. The seaweed salad is optional, but if you can track down wakame (you'll find it in Asian stores) then it's really worth making.*

SEAWEED SALAD (OPTIONAL)

15 g (½ oz) dried wakame seaweed, rinsed

1 tablespoon mirin

1 tablespoon light soy sauce

pinch of white pepper

½ teaspoon toasted sesame seeds

½ teaspoon caster (superfine) sugar

SALSA DRESSING

½ teaspoon grated fresh ginger

juice of 1 lime

1 teaspoon caster (superfine) sugar

½ teaspoon good-quality fish sauce (Three Crabs brand is good)

1 tablespoon olive oil

pinch of salt

pinch of ground white pepper

CHILLI MANGO SALSA

1 fresh mango, or tinned mango (230 g/ 8 oz drained weight), peeled and diced

1 banana shallot, finely chopped

½ red bird's-eye chilli, deseeded and finely chopped

1 tablespoon finely chopped coriander (cilantro) leaves

CRISPY TACOS

20 g (¾ oz) sesame seeds (mixture of white and black)

salt and freshly ground black pepper

200 g (7 oz) sushi-grade tuna fillets

5 tablespoons rapeseed or groundnut oil

6 corn tortillas

¼ white cabbage, finely shredded

TO GARNISH

1 tablespoon fried red onion or shallots (available from most Asian grocers), or home-made (see method on page 55)

Sriracha mayo (see page 241)

fresh coriander (cilantro) leaves, finely chopped

lime wedges

❯ To make the seaweed salad, if using, rehydrate the wakame in tepid water for 5–10 minutes. When it's floppy, drain it. Mix it with the remaining salad ingredients. Set aside.

❯ To make the salsa dressing, mix the ingredients together, stirring to dissolve the sugar.

❯ To make the chilli mango salsa, combine the mango, shallot, chilli and coriander, and then pour the salsa dressing over the mango mixture, and stir.

❯ For the tuna filling, pour the sesame seeds onto a plate with salt and pepper and press the tuna fillets down onto them firmly, to coat. Flip over the fillets and do the same on the other side.

❯ To make the taco shells, heat 4 tablespoons of the oil in a heavy-based frying pan (skillet) over a medium–high heat. Using tongs, place a tortilla in the hot oil. Fry for about 15 seconds, and then flip it over and fold the shell in half, holding it in place with the tongs for about 15 seconds until it's crispy and holding its shape. Drain on kitchen paper, and repeat with the other tortillas. Sprinkle with salt. ⏩➤

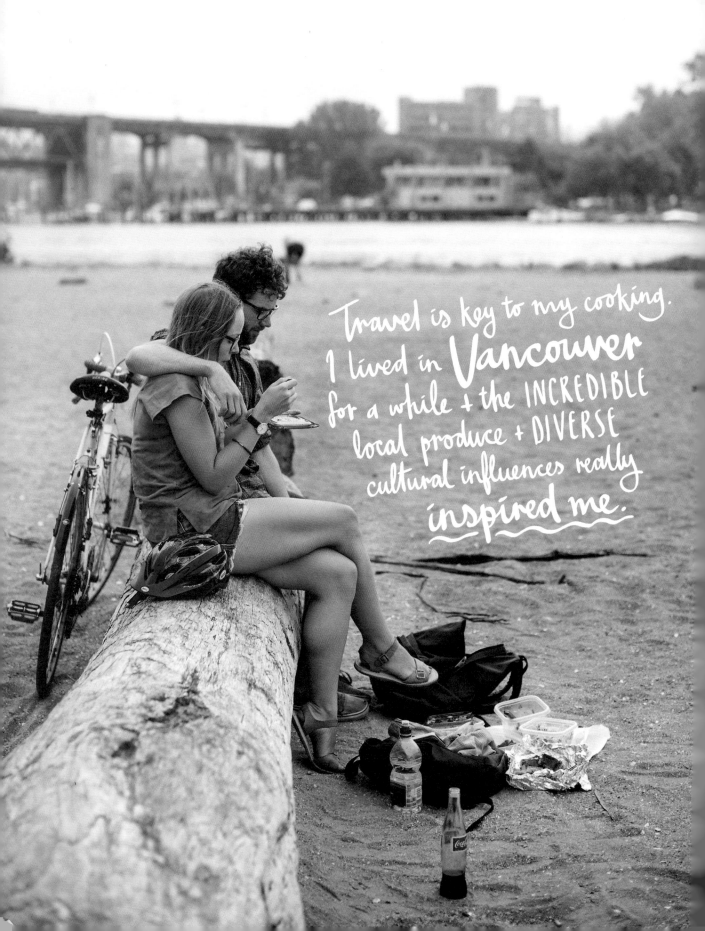

Travel is key to my cooking.
I lived in **Vancouver**
for a while + the INCREDIBLE
local produce + DIVERSE
cultural influences really
inspired me.

> To sear the tuna, heat the remaining tablespoon of oil in the frying pan. When it's really hot, cook the tuna for just over 1 minute on each side, for medium-rare, 1 minute longer for well-done. Remove from the heat, rest for a minute and cut into bite-sized cubes.

> If you don't have store-bought crispy fried red onion or shallots for the garnish, heat 2 tablespoons of oil in a frying pan (skillet), and fry a finely sliced shallot until crisp and golden, but not burnt. Drain on kitchen paper and set aside.

> To assemble the tacos: place some cabbage in each shell, followed by the seaweed salad (if using), mango salsa, tuna and fried shallots. Drizzle over some Sriracha mayo, garnish with coriander leaves and serve with wedges of lime. Eat immediately with your hands.

> **TIP:** To get a nice drizzle effect with the mayonnaise, it's worth investing in a squeezy plastic bottle. They're super cheap, easy to come by in kitchenware stores or on the internet, and will help you get that restaurant look.

Bavette carpaccio with fried capers + mustard mayo

Because you cook the bavette cut in a flash, keeping it rare and juicy inside, it works very well in this version of the Italian classic of beef carpaccio. I discovered this after cooking the Bavette and chips recipe on page 118 and being left with more steak than we could eat. I sliced the chilled leftover meat into super-thin ruby-red slivers and sprinkled it with chopped parsley, fried capers and Parmesan. It went down very well, and has become a firm favourite in our house, especially for laid-back lunches with lots of different salads. The Italians might use rocket (arugula) to top authentic carpaccio, but this being entirely inauthentic, I like to use peppery parsley and mustard mayo for an English twist.

350–400 g (12–14 oz) bavette or skirt steak, or cold, leftover meat from Bavette and chips with bottarga butter and grilled baby gem (see page 118)

sea salt and freshly ground black pepper

flavourless oil (groundnut or sunflower)

1 tablespoon capers, drained

1 tablespoon pine nuts

1 tablespoon English mustard

3 tablespoons mayonnaise

1 tablespoon extra-virgin olive oil, plus extra for frying and drizzling

2 tablespoons freshly squeezed lemon juice

2 tablespoons finely chopped flat-leaf parsley leaves

5 g (¼ oz) Parmesan shards (use a vegetable peeler to make these)

pine nuts, toasted

> If cooking from scratch, season both sides of the steak thoroughly with salt and pepper. Heat a greased heavy-based frying pan (skillet) until stinking hot. Put the steak in the pan (it should sizzle immediately) and cook for about 3–5 minutes on each side for rare-medium. Transfer to a chopping board and leave to rest. Once cooled, refrigerate for 1 hour.

> Heat a little flavourless oil in a frying pan over a medium heat and fry the capers for a few minutes until crisp and puffed. Remove to a bowl covered with kitchen paper. Wipe the pan with kitchen paper and toast the pine nuts for a few minutes, shaking the pan occasionally, until golden brown. Remove from the heat and set aside.

> Whisk together the mustard, mayonnaise and olive oil until you have a loose sauce. Remove the steak from the fridge and finely slice it into slivers against the grain. Arrange on a large plate or serving platter. Drizzle with the mustard mayo and lemon juice, and scatter over the parsley, Parmesan shards and capers. Drizzle with olive oil and finish with the pine nuts and salt and pepper.

SERVES
2 as a starter,
1 as a main

Crab + tarragon mezzaluna

Much to my family's annoyance, my dad always claimed to be indifferent to pasta. But I like to think if he'd tasted this supple, tarragon-flecked fresh pasta, stuffed with crab meat, cloaked in lemon butter and served with shaved asparagus and Parmesan, he might just have been converted. This one's for him. These little filled pasta mezzaluna or 'half moons' take some effort, but making pasta is so satisfying, and these are very rewarding once you taste them, making for a really impressive starter (I once made them for a Come Dine with Me-style feature for Grazia magazine). They're best eaten fresh but do freeze well if you want to make them ahead. Just remove them from the freezer, drop them straight into plenty of very salty boiling water and finish them as below.

CRAB & TARRAGON MEZZALUNA

200 g (7 oz/1⅔ cups) '00' pasta flour (superfine '00' grade), plus extra for dusting

pinch of sea salt

large pinch of dried tarragon

2 eggs, plus 1 egg for egg wash

FILLING

1 shallot, finely chopped

1 tablespoon unsalted butter

80 g (3 oz/½ cup) ricotta

1 whole fresh dressed crab, white and brown meat (150–200 g/5–7 oz, see recipe on page 243)

1 tablespoon freshly squeezed lemon juice

generous pinch of cayenne pepper or, better still, *piment d'espelette*

generous pinch of sea salt

½ teaspoon finely grated lemon zest

TO FINISH

10 g (½ oz) unsalted butter

2 tablespoons freshly squeezed lemon juice

2 asparagus spears, woody base removed, shaved thinly with a mandoline or vegetable peeler

Parmesan shards, to garnish

grated lemon zest

freshly ground black pepper

SPECIAL EQUIPMENT

pasta machine

> Dust a work surface with flour. Sift the flour for the pasta into a large mixing bowl and make a well in the centre. Sprinkle the salt and tarragon onto the flour and crack the eggs into the well. Using the blade of a table knife, break up the egg yolks and, working outwards in a circular motion, start to draw in and incorporate the flour, using the knife blade to mix it all together until you have clumps. Use your fingers to bring it together into a ball, squidging it against any smaller crumbs to incorporate them.

> Once you have a ball, turn it, and any remaining flour, out onto the floured work surface. Knead the dough for 5–10 minutes, pressing and stretching it with the ball of your hand (adding a little more flour if it's still wet and sticky) until it's smooth, soft and springs back into form when squashed. Cut the dough in half to make two balls and wrap them in cling film (plastic wrap). Chill for 1 hour.

> To make the filling, fry the shallot in the butter until soft and then mix with all the remaining filling ingredients in a bowl and season to taste. Set aside.

> Once rested, remove the pasta dough from the cling film and place one of the pasta balls on a floured surface. Press it down with the palm of your hand and roll it out with a floured rolling pin, so that it's thin enough to fit through the thickest setting on the pasta machine and the same width as the pasta machine. Pass the dough through the rollers of the machine on its thickest setting a couple of times, then fold it in half and continue to run it through the pasta machine, gradually reducing the settings ⟫→

to the thinnest setting as you go. Run it through the thinnest setting a couple more times, until it's so fine that you can see your fingers through it, but not so thin that it's drying out and breaking. You don't want to run it through the machine more than 8 times. Lay the sheet of pasta out on the work surface and roll-out the other ball of pasta.

> Once all the dough is rolled and both sheets are on the work surface (each one should be 30–40 cm/12–16 in long), use a pasta cutter, cookie cutter or rim of a large wine glass, around 9–10 cm (3.5–4 inches) in diameter, to cut out circles (or 'mezzaluna') from the sheets of pasta. You should be able to cut 8–10 from each sheet. Spoon the filling in heaped teaspoons onto the centre of the circles. Whisk the egg for the egg wash in a small bowl with 1 tablespoon of water. With your fingertips, dab a little egg wash around the edge of the circle of pasta, fold one half over the other and gently press it down around the filling, pushing out any air and sealing tightly. Use the back of the prongs of a fork to seal the mezzaluna. Place on a floured dish or tray and repeat until you've used up all the pasta and filling.

> For the sauce, melt the butter in a small frying pan (skillet) and squeeze in the lemon juice. Remove from the heat.

> Bring a large saucepan of water to the boil, and add 2 tablespoons of salt (Italian chefs always say that the water you cook pasta in should be as salty as the sea). Drop the mezzaluna in (allow 4–5 mezzaluna per person for a starter, 8–10 for a main) and cook for 2 minutes, or until they float to the surface. Remove them from the water carefully with a slotted spoon and put them into the melted lemon butter, over a medium heat, gently basting the mezzaluna to coat them. Add the asparagus shavings and shake the frying pan, to coat everything in the lemon butter. Divide between plates and top with Parmesan shards and lemon zest. Grind over some black pepper and enjoy!

Keema pau

Dishoom is a London restaurant based on the eccentric, crumbling Irani cafés founded by the Parsi settlers in Mumbai during the 19th century. Fusing elements of Irani and Indian food, these informal eating spaces developed their own unique cuisine. On my travels to Mumbai with the Dishoom crew I was lucky enough to meet the characters that run these special, fading cafés, and one of my favourite dishes was Keema Pau – lusciously oily spiced lamb mince and peas, scooped up with freshly-baked hot buttered toasted bread rolls. Naved Nasir, Dishoom's executive chef, has created his own version, and kindly let me share it here. Although not strictly authentic, I like to eat it with my Cumin brioche (see page 245) in the place of pau: the cumin complements the lamb wonderfully. But if you're short on time, just use store-bought bread rolls or brioche.

25 ml (1 fl oz) vegetable oil

1 large white onion, finely chopped

2 teaspoons ground coriander

1 tablespoon finely grated
fresh ginger

2 garlic cloves, finely chopped

500 g (1 lb 2 oz) lamb mince

1½ teaspoons salt

pinch of plain (all-purpose) flour

2 heaped tablespoons finely
chopped coriander (cilantro) leaves,
plus extra to garnish

2 spring onions (scallions),
finely chopped

1 heaped tablespoon finely
chopped mint leaves

1 small green chilli, finely chopped

50 g (2 oz/¼ cup) plain yoghurt

2 ripe tomatoes, diced

1 bay leaf

50 g (2 oz/scant ½ cup) fresh or
frozen garden peas, cooked

4 Cumin brioche (see page 245)
or 4 soft bread rolls

butter, for spreading

lime wedges, to serve

> Heat the oil in a heavy-based frying pan (skillet) over a medium heat and sauté the onion until golden brown.

> Add the ground coriander, ginger and garlic. Sauté for 3–4 minutes until they start to colour and the oil separates. Add the lamb mince and salt, and fry over a high heat for about 5 minutes until it browns and dries up a little. Add the flour.

> In a bowl, mix together the coriander, spring onion, mint and green chilli to make a coarse paste. Add the yoghurt to the lamb and sauté for a moment, then add the green herb paste and cook for 4–5 minutes until the oil separates. Add the diced tomatoes, bay leaf and peas. Cook for a further 5–8 minutes until the tomatoes are soft.

> Cut the brioche or bread rolls in half and toast until golden brown. Butter while hot.

> Serve the mince in little dishes, garnished with fresh coriander leaves, with the buttered brioche or rolls and wedges of lime alongside. If you like, you can eat this like a sloppy Joe, filling your buns with the mince.

Caramelised cauliflower + cumin soup with cheesy croutons

If you ever find yourself with half a cauliflower lurking in the fridge, this creamy, cumin-spiced soup is one of the tastiest ways of using it up. I like to caramelise the cauliflower to intensify its flavour and add a sweet depth to the soup, which works really nicely with the cumin. I'd favour the wonderful nuttiness of Comté for the croutons if you can find it, otherwise gruyére or Cheddar will do just fine.

big knob of butter

½ large cauliflower

½ large white onion

½ teaspoon cumin seeds

1 potato, peeled and thickly sliced

1 litre (34 fl oz) chicken stock (preferably home-made, (see page 236) but a cube is fine)

1 tablespoon plain natural yoghurt

1 teaspoon freshly squeezed lemon juice

1 teaspoon cider vinegar (optional)

salt and freshly ground black pepper

double (heavy) cream, for drizzling

CHEESY CROUTONS

½ small French baguette, cut into rounds

1 tablespoon olive oil

2 sprigs thyme, leaves picked (optional)

1 teaspoon sea salt

10 g (½ oz) Comté, mature Cheddar or gruyére, finely grated

> Melt the butter in a deep, heavy-based saucepan or cast-iron skillet until sizzling. Turn the heat down to low-medium, add the cauliflower and onion (both cut side down), cover, and leave for about 15 minutes. The sliced side of the cauliflower that's in contact with the pan will gently caramelise, intensifying the nutty flavour of the cauliflower, while the rest of it will steam. The same thing will happen with the onion, making it sweet and soft.

> While the cauliflower and onion are cooking, prepare the croutons. Preheat the oven to 180°C (350°F/Gas 4). Toss the baguette rounds in the olive oil, thyme (if using) and salt in a baking tray until coated, and roast for 5–8 minutes until golden and crunchy (how long this takes will depend on your oven and how thickly you've sliced the bread, so keep an eye on them). Remove from the oven and set aside.

> Uncover the cauliflower and onion pan, and add the cumin seeds and potato slices. Add a little more olive oil if needed and toast for a further 3 minutes, uncovered, flipping the potato slices over once so they are golden brown on both sides. Add the chicken stock and bring to the boil, then turn down to a simmer and cook for 15 minutes.

> Pour the mixture into a large bowl and liquidise with a stick blender, or pop it into a food processor or jug blender and blitz until it's a thick, but not too gloopy, soup. Add the yoghurt and lemon juice and stir in: this will add some acidity, but taste it and if it needs perking up further, add the cider vinegar. Season with salt and pepper and a drizzle of double cream, and stir.

> Preheat the grill. Pour the soup into deep heat-proof bowls, top with the croutons then pile the croutons with the grated cheese. Place under the grill until the cheese has started to bubble, then serve.

Leaving your CLAMS under a gently running tap for 10 MINUTES before you cook them encourages them to give up their GRIT.

Octopus carpaccio with smoked paprika mayo

I have eaten octopus carpaccio – octopus cooked briefly then set in its own gelatine and sliced into delectable wafer-thin slivers – at various restaurants and always marveled at its beauty, elegance and flavour. It makes for an unusual and interesting plate to start a supper, and is perfect for those squeamish people who don't like their cephalopods with tentacles intact. I also assumed it was something that required some kind of seriously high-tech chef kit and skill, but, once I started experimenting with octopus at home, I realised it's actually pretty easy to make – requiring little more than cling film (plastic wrap), a freezer, a bit of patience and a very sharp knife.

1 octopus (about 1 kg/2 lb 3 oz)

1 tablespoon olive oil

1 onion, finely sliced

2 sticks celery, finely chopped

1 carrot, finely chopped

80 ml (2½ fl oz) dry white wine

2 bay leaves

5 g (¼ oz) parsley stalks, tied together with string

3 black peppercorns

star anise

½ lemon

1 tablespoon red wine vinegar

TO GARNISH

1 batch Smoked paprika mayo (see page 241)

extra-virgin olive oil, for drizzling

½ lemon

sea salt and freshly ground black pepper

oregano, chervil leaves or finely chopped flat-leaf parsley leaves

1 tablespoon toasted pine nuts

> First, you need to tenderise the octopus. You can do this easily by freezing it a couple of days before you cook it, and then defrosting it. I tend to buy it frozen from the fishmonger (lots of Asian grocers also sell them frozen) so I just need to defrost it and I'm ready to go. You may also need to remove the eyes. Do this by cutting around and under them with a very sharp knife and popping them and the attached cartilage out. When you cut out the eyes you can then press the hard beak (the creature's mouth) out of the centre cavity where the legs join together. Clean any gunk from the cavities with kitchen paper, and rinse the octopus under cold water for about 10 minutes. You can ask your fishmonger to prepare the octopus for you, but it's good to learn yourself!

> Heat the oil in a deep, heavy-based casserole. Add the onion, celery and carrot, and cook for 5 minutes until soft and aromatic, but not browned. Remove from the heat and wait until the vegetables are completely cool before adding the octopus and all the other ingredients (apart from the garnish). Cover with cold water, bring up to a gentle boil and turn immediately down to a simmer. Cook very gently for 15 minutes.

> Remove the octopus from the bouillon and put it on a chopping board to rest until it's cool enough to handle, but still warm. Lay a large, double sheet of cling film on the work surface. Cut the head off the octopus and tuck it inside the tentacles. Place the octopus on the cling film and wrap one side of the cling film over on top of it. Pull it tightly and, squeezing the octopus together, roll it tightly in the cling film (plastic wrap), twisting the ends so you have a solid octopus 'sausage'. If there is any moisture inside, unravel it, drain out the moisture and repeat the rolling and wrapping – you want a solid mass of octopus that will set in its own gelatine. Allow it to cool then freeze for at least 3 hours, preferably overnight.

> Once the octopus is set, remove the cling film. Using a very sharp knife, carefully slice off wafer-thin slivers. Arrange them on plates, drizzle with the Smoked paprika mayo and olive oil, squeeze over some lemon juice and season with salt and pepper. Garnish with oregano, chervil leaves or parsley, and scatter with toasted pine nuts.

6 little tarts

Chilli crab cocktail tartlets

I love a good crab cocktail, with crunchy lettuce, chilli mayonnaise and spring onion (scallion), but they really have to be made to order (who wants soggy lettuce?) and I don't really want to be faffing around layering lettuce and crab in pretty glasses when I could be drinking wine and gabbing with pals. Which is why I came up with these tasty little tarts, which are perfect made ahead and served chilled, with a crispy green salad on the side. They also make for a perfect packed-lunch treat. There's nothing like a kick of chilli to bring out the sweetness of crab, so I use both Sriracha chilli sauce and fiery bird's-eye red chillies, but you can alter the heat level to suit your taste.

SHORTCRUST PASTRY

225 g (8 oz/1¾ cups) plain (all-purpose) flour, plus extra for dusting

pinch of salt

100 g (3½ oz) chilled unsalted butter, cubed, plus extra for greasing

20 g (¾ oz) chilled lard, cubed

3–4 tablespoons cold water

FILLING

1 whole dressed crab, white and brown meat (180–200 g/6–7 oz, see recipe on page 243)

pinch of sea salt and white pepper

50 g (2 oz) crème fraîche

50 ml (2 fl oz) double (heavy) cream

grated zest and juice of 1 lime

2 teaspoons Sriracha sauce

1 egg, beaten

2 spring onions (scallions), finely chopped

2 red bird's-eye chillies, finely sliced

½ baby gem lettuce, very finely sliced

1 tablespoon sweetcorn kernels (tinned is fine, fresh is better)

1 tablespoon very finely chopped flat-leaf parsley leaves

SPECIAL EQUIPMENT

6 x 10 cm (4 in) loose-bottomed metal tart tins

> To make the pastry, sift the flour and salt into a bowl, add the butter and lard and lightly rub them into the flour until you have a breadcrumb consistency, or whizz the flour and salt briefly with the butter and lard in a food processor then transfer to a bowl. Make a well in the middle and add 3 tablespoons of the water. Mix it in and gather the dough together with one hand to form a ball. If it's too dry, add the remaining water a drop at a time until the dough comes together. Wrap the dough in cling film (plastic wrap) and chill in the fridge for 30 minutes.

> Preheat the oven to 180°C (350°F/Gas 4) and lightly grease the tart tins. Remove the pastry from the fridge, roll it out on a lightly floured surface to 3 mm (¼ in) and line each tin with the pastry. Prick the pastry with a fork, cover the pastry shells with pieces of baking parchment and fill with baking beans. (Scrunch up the baking parchment before you line each case and it will be more pliable and fit more snugly into the holes.) Chill for 15 minutes, then bake blind for 10–12 minutes, until the pastry is turning golden and feels dry. Remove the beans and parchment, and bake for a further 3 minutes. Remove from the oven (keep the oven on) and leave to cool while you make the crab filling.

> Spoon the crab meat into a mixing bowl and carefully check there aren't any pieces of shell. Season with salt and white pepper. Add the crème fraîche, cream, lime juice and zest, Sriracha and egg, and mix vigorously until well combined. Stir through the spring onion, two thirds of the chilli, the lettuce, sweetcorn and parsley. Spoon the filling mix into the cooled tart shells, top with the remaining chilli, and bake for 20–25 minutes, until the crab custard is set. Use a skewer to test this, by inserting it into the filling of one tart. If it comes out clean, they're done. Serve, once cooled, with a crisp green salad.

Dad's seafood sizzle

My mum did most of the cooking in our house, while Dad proudly tended to the vegetable patch. But he did have certain 'signature dishes' as he called them, and this seafood 'sizzle' was one of his finest creations. I remember him getting very excited every time it came to cooking it, prepping all the spring onions (scallions), garlic and chilli meticulously before frying everything together in a lot of olive oil. This is best eaten with big hunks of good bread (we'd always have crusty French baguettes) to soak up the seafood-heady, garlicky oil the seafood should be swimming in. You could add some clams to the mix if you're partial to a mollusc or two.

300 g (10½ oz) fresh
squid, cleaned (ask your
fishmonger to do this
for you)

4 garlic cloves, 2 crushed,
2 finely sliced

salt and freshly ground
black pepper

juice of ½ lemon

150 ml (5 fl oz) light
olive oil

200 g (7 oz) clams,
cleaned (optional)

2 large spring onions
(scallions), cut into
thin matchsticks

1 tablespoon grated
fresh ginger

1 green jalapeno chilli,
finely sliced

2 slices of preserved
lemon, pith and flesh
removed and finely
chopped (optional)

12 shell-on raw
tiger prawns

good-sized French
baguette, torn into chunks

wedges of lemon, to serve

> Marinate the squid for about 1 hour before you cook it: cut the body section of the squid into rectangles (about 5 cm x 3 cm/2 inches x 1¼ inches) and score the underside lightly with a sharp knife in a cross-hatch pattern. Cut the tentacle section of each squid in half. Wash the squid and pat dry carefully with kitchen paper. Put it in a bowl and add the crushed garlic, a pinch of salt, a grind of black pepper, 1 tablespoon of lemon juice and a good glug of the olive oil. Toss it all together so that the squid is well coated in the marinade, cover and chill.

> Half an hour before you cook, take your seafood out of the fridge to let it come to room temperature. If using, put the clams in a bowl under a gently running cold tap for about 10 minutes – this will encourage them to give up their grit.

> Heat 2 tablespoons of oil in a heavy-based non-stick frying pan (skillet). Add the spring onion, ginger, chilli and preserved lemon (if using) and cook for 2 minutes, then add the prawns and sliced garlic. Cook for 2 minutes, shaking the pan to avoid anything catching and burning. When the underside of the prawns start turning pink (you want to see some deep caramelisation on the skins), add the squid and its marinade and shake again, cooking for a further 2 minutes. Add the drained clams, if using, and the rest of the oil and lemon juice, and cover the pan with a lid or plate. Cook for about 3 minutes, shaking the pan to make sure everything cooks evenly, until the clam shells open. If there are any clams that haven't opened after cooking, discard them.

> Spoon into bowls or onto plates, making sure to pour over some of the delicious seafood garlic oil. Serve with chunks of bread, lemon wedges and an extra bowl for the shells.

Leeks vinaigrette

T his is my version of the French bistro classic, which elevates the humble leek to a soft, silky star ingredient bathed in a rich slick of tangy vinaigrette. It's a fantastic dish for vegetarians, and is given added texture and luxury by the toasted walnuts and Gorgonzola.

3 medium leeks, trimmed (dark-green tops and tough outer leaves removed), split in half lengthwise leaving root intact, and rinsed thoroughly

4 tablespoons extra-virgin olive oil

1 teaspoon Dijon mustard

1 tablespoon red wine vinegar

1 garlic clove, crushed

½ teaspoon golden caster (superfine) sugar

1 teaspoon freshly squeezed lemon juice

1 teaspoon finely chopped fresh tarragon

sea salt and freshly ground black pepper

2 tablespoons crumbled Gorgonzola cheese

1 tablespoon walnuts, toasted

› Bring a large pan of salted water to the boil, reduce to a simmer, add the leeks, cover with a cartouche (a piece of greaseproof paper lid with a hole in the middle), and cook for 6 minutes until tender and a deeper green. Test them for tenderness by pressing the tip of a sharp knife into one and pulling it up out of the water – if the leek falls back into the water with no resistance, it's done, if it clings to the knife, let it cook for a little longer. Remove to a bowl of cold water.

› Whisk together the olive oil, Dijon mustard, red wine vinegar, garlic, sugar, lemon juice, tarragon and salt and pepper until emulsified. Taste the vinaigrette and adjust the seasoning/acidity to taste.

› Drain the leeks, place on a serving plate, then drizzle over the vinaigrette. Crumbled over the Gorgonzola and scatter the toasted walnuts on top.

Mexican ceviche with avocado cream

T *hough it's Peruvian in its origins, I really fell in love with ceviche when we were travelling down the coast of Mexico's Yucatan peninsula. Almost anywhere we ate, we'd order this refreshing, spicy dish of fresh fish 'cooked' in a bright citrus marinade and layered up with avocado and red onion – so good eaten with crunchy tortillas and a bit of fiery habanero salsa. This is my version, with the avocado made into a smooth cream which melds with the tangy fish and is just wonderful spread on the crisp tortillas.*

2 very fresh boneless and skinless cod, hake, pollock or coley fillets (200 g/7 oz)

juice of 2 limes, grated zest of 1

grated zest and juice of
½ pink grapefruit

2 teaspoons fish sauce

1 teaspoon caster (superfine) sugar

1 red bird's-eye chilli, very finely chopped

AVOCADO CREAM

1 very ripe avocado

½ shallot

1 tablespoon lime juice, or to taste

pinch of red chilli flakes

1 tablespoon tahini

salt and freshly ground
black pepper

TO SERVE

coriander (cilantro)
leaves, to garnish

black sesame seeds (optional),
for scattering

½ red onion, very finely sliced

extra-virgin olive oil, for drizzling

corn tortillas, fried briefly in oil to
crisp them up, or tortilla chips

➤ Remove any pin bones from your fish fillets, and slice the fillets thinly, across the grain. In a jug, mix together the lime and grapefruit juices and zests, along with the fish sauce, sugar and half the chilli.

➤ Put the fish into the jug and leave for 10–15 minutes, stirring gently once halfway through to evenly coat.

➤ While the fish is marinating, make the avocado cream. Blitz the avocado flesh, shallot, lime juice, chilli flakes and tahini in a food processor and blend until you have a smooth cream. Scrape out of the food processor, and into a bowl, and season to taste.

➤ When the fish is 'cooked' on the outside but still slightly raw inside, remove it from the marinade and arrange on serving plates. Pour over a spoonful of the marinade and spoon little dots of the avocado cream onto the fish. Sprinkle over the coriander and sesame seeds, if using, sliced red onion and remaining chilli. Drizzle over a little extra-virgin olive oil and serve with the tortillas.

Winter squash soup with chipotle, roasted garlic + crunchy seeds

This recipe can be made with pumpkin, or any variety of winter squash, but I really love the red kuri squash for its sweet and nutty flavour. This is a favourite for autumn/winter thanks to its comforting warmth, simplicity and resourcefulness – with its deep orange colour and smoky chipotle heat it's like winter in a bowl. Nothing is wasted here as you use both the soft skin and the crunchy roasted seeds of the squash to add some texture to the soup.

---

5 fat garlic cloves

3 tablespoons extra virgin olive oil, plus extra for coating the squash

1 large red kuri squash or a medium-sized pumpkin

3 teaspoons chipotle chilli powder or cayenne pepper (or to taste)

½ teaspoon sea salt

1 teaspoon garlic granules

knob of butter

sea salt freshly ground black pepper

1 white onion, finely sliced

100 ml (3 ½) white wine vinegar

1 bay leaf

1 litre (34 fl oz) of chicken or vegetable stock (preferably home-made, see page 236, but a cube is fine)

2 tablespoons natural plain yoghurt or cultured buttermilk

Parmesan, grated

› Preheat the oven to 160°C (320°F/Gas 3).

› Wrap the garlic cloves in foil with 1 tablespoon of olive oil. Cut the squash in half and scoop the seeds out into a roasting tin, removing as much of the soft, sticky pulp as you can. Toss the seeds with 1 tablespoon of olive oil, 2 teaspoons of chipotle powder, salt and garlic granules and roast them with the foiled garlic for 20 minutes.

› Rub the squash all over with olive oil, season with salt and pepper and place cut side down on a roasting tray. After 20 minutes add in the squash halves to the oven and roast for a further 35 minutes, or until the flesh of the squash is meltingly tender. Remove the garlic, seeds and squash from the oven and set aside to cool. Chop the squash into chunks. You don't need to discard the skin unless it's tough and the soft flesh is naturally coming away from it.

› Heat the remaining 1 tablespoon of oil and the butter in a heavy-bottomed saucepan and fry your onion slices with the bay leaf, 1 teaspoon of chipotle powder and a pinch of salt until the onions are soft and fragrant. Deglaze with the vinegar.

› Add in the squash, the softened garlic cloves and the stock, and bring to the boil. Simmer for 10–15 minutes. Remove the bay leaf, add in 2 tablespoons of yoghurt or buttermilk and using a stick blender or food processor, purée to a smooth soup consistency, seasoning to taste with salt and pepper. Serve scattered with the crunchy roasted seeds and grated Parmesan.

CHAPTER 3

Snacks + Sides

I HAD TO HAVE A CHAPTER IN THIS BOOK DEDICATED TO SNACKS AND SIDES.

For me, that's where it all begins; when you first start to charm your palate with a little something to – as an old pal of mine from Yorkshire used to say – 'put you on'.

When my friends and I get together, there are always snacks involved. Actually, who am I kidding? When I am alone in the flat working, having a night in with Jamie, or catching up with family, there are snacks involved. There are snacks involved when I have a bath. You get the picture...

While store-bought crisps and dips can be a great time saver, I think it's nice to have some more interesting, accessible home-made nibbles in your recipe arsenal. There's just something a bit more special about kicking off a meal with something you've put together yourself, be it juicy radishes and a salty dip, home-made bread and butter, or something refined like a perfectly crisp, cheesy *gougère*. In this chapter you'll find some ideas for pre-meal munchies using fresh, fridge and store-cupboard ingredients you're likely to have to hand, many of which can be whipped up in no time at all.

One of the best tongue teasers I can remember eating was during my first trip to Mexico. It was our first day in the scorching heat of the beautiful Yucatán coast, where crumbling Mayan ruins overlook warm crystal waters and iguanas lounge lazily on every available surface. We were hot, and boy, were we hungry. So we stopped at the side of the road for some fish tacos and cold Cokes from a street food van. As soon as we sat down on the high stools by the service hatch, the chef handed us little plastic cups filled with a bright coral-coloured, pungent smelling broth. He

then passed out a little plate with chunks of lime, chopped white onion, chilli and coriander (cilantro).

I looked at the other customers and copied what they were doing: squeezing in the lime, chucking in some onion and coriander. I took a sip and – I am salivating even thinking about this – my mouth was filled with the most beautifully intense, heady seafood broth, deeply spicy with Mexican chillies and nutty with roasted prawn shells. The raw onions added a gorgeous juicy crunch and the coriander an aromatic freshness.

Sensing my delight, the Mexican man next to me explained what I was eating, 'It's *caldo de camarón*,' he purred, smiling, 'Betterrr than Viagra'. I got the feeling he knew what he was talking about. As soon as I'd tasted it I was hooked. We returned to that same van about four times before we left Playa Del Carmen, just for this soup – though the tacos were good too.

That chef had it sussed, balancing spice, salt, sweet and sour along with a winning confluence of textures and temperatures in his opening dish. And that's just what a good snack should do – pique your palate and immediately seduce you. There needs to be a party in your mouth, but it doesn't need to be something too heavy, complicated or expensive. Because you eat these pre-meal nibbles in small, bite-sized quantities, they're a great way to play with bold, intense flavours, so you can really have some fun with them and get creative.

My kind of bagna càuda

*A*uthentic bagna càuda ('hot bath') is a local speciality in Piedmont, Italy, where it's served warm with raw, boiled or roasted vegetables to plunge into it, sometimes with the addition of cream or bread to thicken it. My interpretation of this intense anchovy- and garlic-based dip uses less oil and butter than the Piedmontese version, and some cannellini beans to thicken it, but it's not for the faint-hearted. It's easy to whip up with store-cupboard ingredients, making a great improvised starter for impromptu dinners, picnics or barbecues. I like to serve it with a glittering array of crunchy veg, which offset its pungency, but it's also rather good with cold roast pork. Vary what you serve with it according to what's in season, but it's particularly good with sweet carrots, creamy, bitter chicory and peppery, juicy radish.

---

10 garlic cloves, peeled

300 ml (10 fl oz) whole milk

15 good-quality salt-packed anchovy fillets, rinsed and finely chopped , or failing that, good-quality jarred anchovies in oil

25 g (1 oz) unsalted butter

½ x 400 g (14 oz) tin cannellini beans, drained

1 tablespoon double (heavy) cream

3 teaspoons red wine vinegar

2 tablespoons extra-virgin olive oil

juice of ½ lemon

freshly ground black pepper

TO SERVE
*(vary this according to
what's in season)*

breakfast radishes, rinsed

romanesco cauliflower
(or regular cauliflower), broken
into florets and blanched in boiling
salted water for 2 minutes

red or white chicory leaves

fennel bulb, rinsed and sliced

baby carrots, rinsed and trimmed

courgette (zucchini) flowers
(when in season)

> In a bowl, cover the garlic cloves with 100 ml (3½ fl oz) of the milk, and soak for 1 hour. Discard the milk and put the soaked garlic cloves in a saucepan. Cover with the remaining milk and 1 tablespoon of water. Cook very gently, part-covered with a lid, over a very low heat for about 20 minutes, until the garlic is soft enough to mush into the milk (but don't mush them in now, as you will blend the dip later).

> Add the chopped anchovies and cook, stirring, until the anchovies have dissolved. Add the butter and stir until melted. Transfer to a food processor and blitz with the drained beans, cream, vinegar and olive oil until smooth. Transfer to a bowl and add the lemon juice and black pepper to taste, and more olive oil, if you wish. Serve warm, or at room temperature, with the prepared vegetables alongside. The dip will keep for a couple of days covered in the fridge, and is great stirred into pasta or eaten with cold-cuts.

Romesco sauce with grilled spring onions

This sweet, smoky, nutty Catalan sauce is often an accompaniment to grilled fish and seafood or calçot onions in Spain, but it's also a favourite of mine for snacking when I have friends round, and it's especially good to have at a barbecue, its sweetness pairing well with charred ingredients. I tend to buy a big jar of grilled red peppers (capsicums) from my local Turkish store and keep them in the fridge just for this, as I find they work just as well as grilling the peppers yourself, and they have an added acidity from their preserving juice. The sauce keeps well for up to 2–3 days in the fridge, so it's a good one to make ahead. Try and use the best olive oil you can find for this, to really make it sing.

50 g (2 oz/⅓ cup) roasted hazelnuts

50 g (2 oz/⅓ cup) blanched almonds, washed

2 garlic cloves, peeled

400 g (14 oz) skinned roasted red peppers (capsicums) from a jar

1 teaspoon good-quality tomato purée

1 slice of slightly stale sourdough bread

80 ml (2½ fl oz) good-quality extra-virgin olive oil, plus extra for griddling

sea salt and freshly ground black pepper

½ teaspoon cayenne pepper

½ teaspoon hot smoked paprika (*pimenton*)

2–4 teaspoons red wine vinegar

bunch of the freshest spring onions (scallions) you can find, papery outer layer removed

> Put the nuts in the bowl of the food processor with the garlic, and blitz until you have coarse crumbs. Add the red peppers, and blitz again to a coarse paste, then add the tomato purée, sourdough and a glug of the oil to loosen the mixture, and blitz once more until you have a smoother paste. Pour the sauce into a mixing bowl and season with the salt, black pepper, cayenne pepper and paprika. Pour in the rest of the olive oil, stirring vigorously to incorporate it. Add the vinegar 1 teaspoon at a time, until the sauce has the right acidity – it should make you salivate!

> For the spring onions, simply brush them with a little olive oil, season them with salt, and griddle or barbecue them over a high heat, turning them occasionally, until they are softening at the core and have black char marks all over them. Dip them into the sauce and enjoy.

My favourite lentils

Puy lentils are my fave, and I've been known to eat my way through an entire pan of this dish in one sitting. Great on their own, or topped with a poached egg and some pickled ceps for a light lunch, these lentils are also gorgeous with roasted meats like the Porchetta on page 154, or eaten cold to bulk-out salads. You can serve them warm, but I'm rather partial to them at room temperature.

extra-virgin olive oil

knob of butter

2 medium white onions, finely sliced

1 carrot, finely chopped

2 garlic cloves, crushed

2 bay leaves

4 black peppercorns

½ teaspoon salt

300 g (10½ oz/1¾ cups) puy or other green lentils, rinsed and drained

juice of ½ lemon

sea salt and freshly ground black pepper

> Heat 1 tablespoon of olive oil and the butter in a non-stick frying pan (skillet) over a low heat, and fry the onions very gently for about 15 minutes, without browning them, until soft and sweet. Set aside.

> In a saucepan, heat a little olive oil and gently sauté the carrot and garlic for about 3 minutes. Add the bay leaves, peppercorns, salt and lentils, cover with 500 ml (17 fl oz) water and bring to the boil. Reduce and simmer, covered, for about 30 minutes, or until the lentils have absorbed all the liquid and are tender. If they dry out at any point, just add a bit more water.

> Once cooked, stir through the onion, 2 tablespoons of olive oil and the lemon juice, and season to taste. Remove the bay leaves and peppercorns before serving.

Cumin + garlic black beans

This little recipe is one of my best-loved side dishes when I'm making anything Mexican. It's lovely as an accompaniment to the Melting Mexican pulled pork tacos (see page 164) or Chipotle roast chicken (see page 163), but also great on its own loaded onto tacos and topped with a poached egg as a quick and satisfying lunch or light supper.

1 tablespoon olive oil

1 white onion, finely chopped

2 garlic cloves, crushed

salt and freshly ground black pepper

400 g (14 oz) tin black beans

2 teaspoons ground cumin

juice of 1 lime

coriander (cilantro) leaves, to garnish

lime wedges, to serve

red chilli flakes or chopped fresh red chilli, to serve (optional)

➤ Heat the olive oil in a non-stick frying pan over a low heat, and fry the onion and garlic for about 3–5 minutes with a pinch of salt and pepper, until soft but not browned. Remove from the heat.

➤ Drain the black beans in a sieve, reserving the juice, and rinse them under cold water. Put three quarters of the beans in a food processor with 2 tablespoons of their tin juice, and blitz them to a purée. Pour them into the pan with the onion and garlic, adding the cumin, lime juice and a slosh more olive oil, and return to a medium heat for 2 minutes. Add the remaining whole beans to the pan and warm through, checking for seasoning and adding more salt if needed. Garnish with chopped coriander and serve with lime wedges for squeezing over. If you like, you could add red chilli flakes or chopped fresh chilli at the end for a bit of heat.

Baba ganoush

*T*his is a really simple, but deliciously smoky Middle Eastern aubergine (eggplant) dip that can be made ahead and kept in the fridge for a few days – the flavours improve with time. It's great with the Cheat's seeded crackers (see below), or with cumin-spiced lamb kebabs and toasted pitta. I like to add a little pomegranate molasses to give it a fruity, acidic depth.

2 medium aubergines (eggplants), rinsed

2 tablespoons creamy Greek yoghurt

2 teaspoons tahini

1 garlic clove, crushed

2 tablespoons chopped coriander (cilantro) leaves, plus extra to garnish

1 teaspoon pomegranate molasses

½ teaspoon ground cumin

pinch of ground white pepper

large pinch of sea salt

2 tablespoons freshly squeezed lemon juice

olive oil, to drizzle

➤ Pierce the skin of the aubergines all over with a fork and rest them over a steady gas flame or glowing barbecue, rotating occasionally, for 10–15 minutes, until they're collapsing inside. Leave to cool. Peel away the black, hard skin and scoop the soft, luscious flesh into the bowl of a food processor. Add all the other ingredients and blitz until you have a chunky, thick paste. Drizzle with olive oil and garnish with coriander leaves.

Cheat's seeded crackers

*T*hese crunchy cheat's crackers will be your friend for life. They will repeatedly save your bacon when you have friends coming over and only a packet of tortillas turning crusty in the fridge. Aside from being a brilliant way to use up surplus tortillas, these little belters are great with dips, and deceptively easy to make, though they give the impression you've gone to quite a lot of trouble. I've used chia seeds on top because they're packed full of omega-3 fatty acids and help aid digestion, and also cumin and the Middle Eastern spice mix of za'atar, but you could play around with the flavours and try onion or poppy seeds, or even fennel or coriander seeds.

1 egg

1 tablespoon ground cumin

pinch of red chilli flakes

sea salt and freshly ground black pepper

5 wheat or durum tortillas

1 tablespoon chia seeds (available from most health-food stores)

1 tablespoon za'atar spice mix

SPECIAL EQUIPMENT

pastry brush

➤ Preheat the oven to 180°C (350°F/Gas 4).

➤ Beat the egg with the ground cumin, chilli flakes, and a little salt and pepper. Use a pastry brush to brush the spiced egg wash over the tortillas. Scatter with chia seeds and za'atar, then cut each tortilla into triangles with scissors. Bake for about 10 minutes until crisp and golden, turning them over halfway through cooking. Keep a really close eye on them when you're baking them though, as they can easily burn because they're so thin.

Baby potato + rosemary pizzas

I first had potato pizza in Rome, where you can buy it by the freshly-baked, crispy potato and olive-oil-laden slice at any pizza stall worth its salt. Some people might baulk at the thought of carb-on-carb pizza, but I've always been fond of the odd chip butty, and I love the simplicity of this dish: it's the ultimate comfort food. The combination of woody rosemary with garlic, earthy potato, soft dough and crunchy sea salt is a humble delight.

350 g (12 oz/3 cups) strong plain (all-purpose) flour, plus extra for dusting

1 teaspoon caster (superfine) sugar

1 teaspoon salt

½ x 7 g (¼ oz) sachet fast-action dried yeast

225 ml (8 fl oz) lukewarm water

10–12 baby potatoes, washed and drained

1 garlic clove, crushed

4 tablespoons mascarpone, plain natural yoghurt or crème fraîche

extra-virgin olive oil

4 sprigs thyme, leaves picked

4 sprigs rosemary, leaves picked

sea salt and freshly ground black pepper

> Dust a clean work surface with flour. Sift the flour, sugar, salt and yeast into a large mixing bowl. Add the water and mix to form a loose dough. Turn it out onto the floured surface, bring together any crumbs and knead for about 10 minutes, until smooth and elastic. You could do this in a stand mixer fitted with a dough hook instead, if you have one. Shape into a ball and put in an oiled bowl. Cover with a tea towel or cling film (plastic wrap) and leave for about 1 hour in a warm place until it's doubled in size.

> Preheat the oven to 220°C (425°F/Gas 7) and put 2 baking trays in the oven to heat up (or a pizza stone, if you have one). Knead the dough again until smooth and divide it with a sharp knife into two or four balls. Weigh each ball if you want to be precise. Dust a rolling pin with flour, flatten the dough balls with the palm of your hand, and roll them out into thin pizza bases (I like long rectanglar ones), rotating and stretching until you have your desired size and thickness. Don't worry too much about being neat!

> Using a mandoline or a sharp knife, slice the potatoes very thinly, and pat away any excess moisture with a clean tea towel. Mix the garlic clove with the crème fraîche, yoghurt or mascarpone. Just before you're ready to assemble your topping, toss the potatoes in a generous glug of olive oil with the thyme, rosemary, and some sea salt and black pepper. Spoon some of the creamy mixture onto your bases and spread to cover them using the back of the spoon. Lay the potato slices over the pizzas and top with any remaining herbs and olive oil from the bowl. Take the hot baking trays (or the pizza stone) out of the oven, flour them and transfer the bases to the trays with a large spatula. Bake for 16–20 minutes, until the crust is puffed and golden and the potatoes are crisping up around the edges. Repeat with the other pizza(s). Devour.

The combination of woody ROSEMARY with garlic, earthy POTATO, soft dough + sea salt is a *humble delight*

Broccoflower cheese pies

I am a little bit in love with romanesco cauliflower (also known as broccoflower). It is, to me, the most beautiful brassica of them all. Having first spotted it while working in Italy where it beautifies many a fresh-food market stall, I now buy it whenever I see it. Visually and texturally, it's a feast: its swirling green florets a cross between broccoli and cauliflower, and it works with the same ingredients as its siblings, being especially compatible with strong hard cheese. If you can't find romanesco, these little pies work just as well with cauliflower, or broccoli, or a mixture of both.

1 batch shortcrust pastry (see page 75), chilled

butter, for greasing

plain (all-purpose) flour, for dusting

1 romanesco cauliflower, cut into little florets (discard the stalk)

3 eggs

150 g (5 oz/generous cup) pecorino, Gruyère or other similarly potent hard cheese, finely grated

30 g (1 oz/¼ cup) finely grated Parmesan, plus more to finish

30 ml (1 fl oz) double (heavy) cream

150 ml (5 fl oz) whole milk

pinch of red chilli flakes

salt and freshly ground black pepper

SPECIAL EQUIPMENT

12-hole muffin tin

> Preheat the oven to 180°C (350°F/Gas 4) and lightly grease the muffin tin. Roll out the chilled pastry on a lightly floured work surface to 2–3 mm (⅛ in) thick and cut out rounds slightly bigger than the holes in the muffin tin. Line each hole with the pastry so that it's level with the top of each hole.

> Chill the pastry for 15 minutes, then use a fork to prick the base of each case. Line with pieces of baking parchment and fill with baking beans. (Scrunch up the baking parchment before you line each case and it will be more pliable and fit more snugly into the holes.) Bake 'blind' for 10–12 minutes. Remove from the oven, remove the beans and parchment, and bake for a further 3 minutes to avoid a soggy bottom. Remove from the oven (keep the oven on) and leave to cool while you make the filling.

> Blanch the romanesco florets in salted boiling water for barely 1 minute – just until it turns bright green – and drain.

> Crack the eggs into a mixing bowl and add the cheeses, cream, milk and chilli flakes. Season with salt and pepper, and whisk to combine. Divide the filling between the cooled pastry cases, leaving about 1 cm (½ in) of space to add the romanesco and allow for the custard to expand.

> Arrange the romanesco in the filling, keeping half of it above the filling for presentation (you want to see those gorgeous florets!) and grate over a little bit more Parmesan. Bake for 15–20 minutes, or until the custard is set and the pastry is golden and crisp. Cool on a wire rack.

Marmite gougères

Essentially a low-brow British take on a sophisticated French classic, this really works. Marmite – a thick, black, sticky yeast extract – is one of my all-time favourite comfort foods, and a British cult product you either love or loathe. As kids, we would have it spread sparingly onto hot buttered toast every morning – its tar-like, umami slick melding with the melted butter and oozing into the white crumb. If we felt ill, or blue, or just plain hungry, we'd reach for the Marmite, and it always hit the spot. One day my sister Alice, herself a bit of a maverick in the kitchen, came up with the genius idea of putting it on her cheese on toast: life was never the same again. I've translated that combination to these indulgent choux pastry puffs. If you can't find Marmite (though I have tracked it down in Canada and the US), try Vegemite, or omit it altogether – you'll still get gorgeous gougères.

120 g (4 oz) unsalted butter

150 ml (5 fl oz) whole milk

1½ tablespoon Marmite

150 g (5 oz/1 cup) plain (all-purpose) flour, sifted

4 eggs

100 g (3½ oz) Cheddar, grated, plus 1 tablespoon more for scattering

1 teaspoon cayenne pepper

big pinch of freshly ground black pepper

½ teaspoon freshly grated nutmeg

SPECIAL EQUIPMENT

piping bag and 1 cm (½ in) round nozzle

❯ Preheat the oven to 200°C (400°F/Gas 6) and line 2 large baking sheets with baking parchment.

❯ Heat the butter, milk and Marmite with 75 ml (2½ fl oz) water in a medium saucepan until the butter is completely melted, the Marmite has dissolved and the mixture has just reached boiling point. Tip in the flour and beat very quickly with a wooden spoon, over the heat, until you have a smooth mixture the consistency of mashed potato, which comes away from the sides of the pan. Transfer the mixture to a mixing bowl and allow to cool for 1 minute. Now add 1 egg, beating it into the mixture until completely incorporated – initially it will separate the mixture and go sloppy, but keep beating and it will mix in. Repeat this process with the remaining 3 eggs, one after the other, until the dough is thick, smooth and shiny. Stir in the grated cheese, peppers and nutmeg.

❯ Spoon the mixture into the piping bag fitted with a nozzle. Pipe little round mounds (about the size of a chestnut) onto the trays, leaving space between each mound to allow for rising. If you don't have a piping bag, just spoon teaspoons of the mixture onto the tray. Scatter over the remaining Cheddar. Bake for 20–25 minutes, until puffed and golden. Serve warm, or cool on a wire rack and reheat in a 180°C (350°F/Gas 4) oven for a few minutes until they crisp up. These gougères can be made in advance and frozen once cool, ready to be crisped up in a hot oven at your convenience.

Chilli, garlic + sesame kale chips

I t's a bit of a cliché, but I got really into kale chips while living in Vancouver, where there's a penchant for things of the healthy, hippy, handmade variety. Suffice to say, kale is big, and kale chips are the snack of choice. I'll admit I was cynical at first, but once I'd felt the impossibly light, savoury shatter of one of these green crisps on my tongue, I forgot my British scepticism and started filling my repurposed cotton shopping bag with bunches of the stuff like everyone else. The trick to making these successfully is to make sure the kale is dry before you cook it, and to not use too much oil. Play around with how you season them: I sometimes like to add crushed roasted hazelnuts or cumin into the mix, but this is my basic recipe.

---

200 g (7 oz) kale, rinsed, dried, thick stems removed and leaves torn into crisp-sized pieces

½ tablespoon rapeseed or groundnut oil

2 teaspoons red chilli flakes

1 tablespoon garlic granules

1 tablespoon black and white sesame seeds

large pinch of sea salt

❯ Preheat the oven to 160°C (320°F/Gas 3). Toss the kale lightly in the oil, chilli, garlic, sesame seeds and salt, and arrange in one layer on baking trays or roasting tins: you'll probably need to use more than one – you don't want them to be crowded as then the kale won't crisp up properly. Roast for 12–15 minutes, until crisp but still green rather than brown. Turn the oven off and leave them in the oven for 5 minutes, with the oven door closed, to cool and crisp up.

CHAPTER 4

Bigger plates
+ super suppers

A RETURN TO CARNIVOROUS CULINARY RESOURCEFULNESS HAS MARKED A TASTY SHIFT FOR MODERN COOKS.

Chefs like Fergus Henderson and April Bloomfield have shown that using as much of the animal as possible is not just the honourable way to cook meat if you eat it, it's the smartest way, too. In this and the next chapter, where I share my recipes for my favourite bigger plates, suppers and feasts, I encourage you to cook with underused, cheaper cuts of meat that should be celebrated through crafty cooking, rather than wasted. Cuts like ballsy bavette or oomph-filled oxtail are brilliant because as well as being cheaper than prime cuts, they yield amazing flavours when cooked to their best.

You'll probably need to go to the butcher to source these cuts, and it's entirely up to you, but I'd encourage you to use a butcher for most of your meat shopping anyway, because they tend to hang meat properly (improving flavour and tenderness), and will be able to tell you all sorts of useful things about it, like where it's from and different ways to cook it. They might even save you a fair few pennies in the process.

In this chapter, you'll find dishes that can be thrown together in no time at all for when you're in a hurry, and some that you need to spend more time on, but which bring rewarding results, like the sumptuous Oxtail French dip sandwich (see page 115) – a warm 'project sandwich' with the bonus of accompanying gravy for dipping. With some of these recipes, you'll notice that the razzle dazzle comes in the final flourish or finishing touch – a melting disc of deeply savoury bottarga butter here, a handful of crushed, toasted hazelnuts there.

And it's not just meat that offers us a diversity of cuts, as top British chef James Lowe shows us with his pan-fried Cod cheeks recipe on page 123. While some of these recipes, such as the Parsley, bacon and broad bean risotto (see page 112), rely on more economical ingredients, they don't lack flavour or luxury in the eating, so there's no need to feel like you're being austere or denying yourself a thing. On the contrary, I hope these recipes will delight and entice you, and encourage you to go a little off-piste with some everyday ingredients.

Mushroom ragu with truffled polenta

T his wow-factor meat-free supper is so easy to throw together. The dried mushrooms add an intense depth along with the broth you rehydrate them in. To make this totally vegetarian use vegetable stock or water for the polenta, instead of chicken stock.

MUSHROOM RAGU

15 g (½ oz/¾ cup) dried mushrooms (porcini, ceps, chanterelle, oriental varieties or, even better, a mix of all)

1 tablespoon olive oil

1 garlic clove, finely chopped

3 shallots, diced

knob of butter

1–2 sprigs thyme

250 g (9 oz) fresh mushrooms such as chestnut, shiitake, portobello and white – the bigger ones broken into chunks (I use wild when I can find them)

sea salt and freshly ground black pepper

1 teaspoon finely chopped fresh tarragon or ¼ teaspoon dried tarragon

½ medium glass of dry white wine

20 g (¾ oz) flat-leaf parsley, leaves only, finely chopped, plus extra for garnish

dash of tarragon vinegar or freshly squeezed lemon juice

POLENTA

300 ml (10 fl oz) chicken stock (preferably home-made, see page 236, but a cube is fine)

generous pinch of salt

1 bay leaf

100 ml (3½ fl oz) whole milk

80 g (3 oz) polenta

1 tablespoon mascarpone or butter

15 g (½ oz) grated Parmesan, plus extra to garnish

1 tablespoon good-quality truffle oil

crème fraîche or mascarpone, to serve (optional)

> Put the dried mushrooms in a bowl and cover with 30 ml (1 fl oz) boiling water. Leave them to soak for 10–15 minutes while you prepare the polenta.

> Put the chicken stock, salt, bay leaf and milk in a saucepan and bring to the boil. Once it's boiling, begin to gently whisk and slowly, steadily pour in the polenta until it's all combined. Turn the heat down to a simmer and cook, stirring with a wooden spoon occasionally, for 30 minutes, or until the polenta has absorbed all the liquid and is creamy and soft (if you're using quick-cook polenta, remove the pan from the heat 1 minute after you've stirred it in). If it's too thick and not wet enough, just add more water to loosen it – it should be the consistency of runny potato purée. Once cooked and thick and creamy, stir in the mascarpone (or butter), Parmesan and truffle oil, and leave in a warm place until you're ready to serve.

> For the mushroom ragu, heat the oil in a frying pan (skillet) and add the garlic and shallots, stirring and cooking gently for about 4 minutes until soft and aromatic. Turn up the heat, add the butter and thyme, and start adding the fresh mushrooms, breaking up the bigger ones into the frying pan, coating them in the butter and garlic and onion mixture. Season with salt and pepper and cook the mushrooms for 8–10 minutes until their juices start releasing and evaporating, and they are caramelising and crisping up slightly (to intensify their flavour). Depending on the size of your pan, you may need to do this in batches. When the mixture is fairly dry, add the tarragon, wine, rehydrated mushrooms and mushroom stock (passed through a fine sieve) and cook gently for 10 minutes. Transfer to a metal bowl and check for seasoning, then add the parsley and a dash of vinegar or lemon juice for acidity.

> Divide the warm polenta between 2 bowls and top with the mushroom ragu. Garnish with chopped parsley, Parmesan, and if you like, some crème fraîche or mascarpone.

MAKES
**4 as a starter,
2 as a main**

Parsley, bacon + broad bean risotto

T his pretty green risotto is a frugal but delightful dish to cook for loved ones. It uses economical ingredients in a refined way, and melds harmonious flavours that will have you begging for seconds. Taking the traditional flavour combination of broad (fava) beans and parsley, it ramps it up a notch by adding salty bacon and rich risotto. Try to find the smallest, newest broad beans you can for this.

150 g (5 oz/1 cup) shelled fresh or frozen broad (fava) beans

50 g (2 oz) spinach leaves

60 g (2 oz) flat-leaf parsley leaves

3 tablespoons olive oil, plus extra for frying (if necessary)

10 g (½ oz) butter

4 rashers (slices) good-quality smoked streaky bacon, cut into lardons or strips

1 onion, finely chopped

salt and freshly ground black pepper

1 sprig thyme, leaves picked

1 large garlic clove, finely chopped

150 g (5 oz/scant ¾ cup) arborio risotto rice

75 ml (2½ fl oz) dry white wine

750 ml (25 fl oz) warm chicken stock (preferably home-made, see page 236, but a cube is fine)

20 g (¾ oz) grated Parmesan, plus extra to garnish

1 tablespoon freshly squeezed lemon juice

❯ Blanch the broad beans in a pan of boiling salted water for a couple of minutes, until al dente. Remove with a slotted spoon to a bowl of iced water, and peel them (if the skins are tough). Using the same boiling water, blanch the spinach and parsley until wilted but still bright green. Remove from the pan with a slotted spoon, leave to cool for a moment and squeeze out the excess water. Transfer the spinach and parsley to a food processor or mini-chopper (or use a stick blender) with 2 tablespoons of the olive oil and 1 teaspoon of water and blitz to a fine purée. Set aside.

❯ Heat the remaining oil and half the butter in a large non-stick frying pan (skillet) or heavy-based saucepan and fry the bacon for about 5 minutes until it starts crisping up. Its fat will have melted out into the pan. Remove the bacon with a slotted spoon.

❯ Add the onion to the pan with a good grind of black pepper and the thyme, coating it in the fat and scraping up any crusty bits from the bottom of the frying pan. Cook over a medium heat. You want it soft but not browned. Add the garlic and stir. Add a slosh more olive oil if the pan is looking dry, then add the rice, stirring to coat it in the oil and cook for a couple of minutes, until it turns translucent. Pour in the white wine, which will deglaze the pan and start to evaporate almost instantly. Stir to incorporate, and cook for 2 minutes until it has mostly evaporated, and then add 1 ladleful of the warm stock and stir until absorbed.

❯ Continue this process a ladleful at a time, for 20–30 minutes, stirring continually, until all the stock is absorbed, and the rice is creamy but still a little al dente and retaining a little bite, but with no hard chalky core. Take the pan off the heat and stir through the Parmesan and the remaining butter, and then the parsley and spinach purée, stirring thoroughly to incorporate it and create a vivid green risotto. Stir through the crispy bacon, broad beans and lemon juice, and season to taste.

❯ Serve immediately with grated Parmesan.

Oxtail French dip sandwich

This is what my pal Helen Graves, ace food writer and self-styled sandwich expert would call a 'project sandwich': it takes a lot of making, but is totally worth the effort. After a trip to LA where I ate at Philippe's – the original purveyors of French dip (a roasted meat baguette dipped in the roasting juices) – I started a short-lived French dip sandwich stall in Brixton with my mate Andrew Dolleymore. Before life took over and we had to put our street food ambitions to one side, we had a few successful runs where people queued for our roast beef 'double dip' – it was a hit! This version uses oxtail, a cheap, flavoursome cut which creates the richest, most delicious gravy enriched with melted fat and gelatine, for extreme dippage. I like to add spiced pickled beetroots (beets) and red onion for a sweet, acidic kick and a bit of colour, but any pickle you might have lying around will do nicely.

---

1 kg (2 lb 3 oz) meaty oxtail, trimmed of excess fat – get your butcher to cut it into 4–5 cm (1½ –2 in) slices

sea salt and freshly ground black pepper

2 teaspoons garlic granules

1 tablespoon rapeseed, vegetable or sunflower oil

1 tablespoon olive oil

1 medium white onion, chopped

2 carrots, roughly chopped

2 sticks celery, chopped

2 bay leaves

700 ml (24 fl oz) red wine

1 star anise

200 ml (7 fl oz) chicken stock (preferably home-made, see page 236, but a cube is fine)

1 tablespoon softened butter

2 tablespoons plain (all-purpose) flour

1–2 teaspoons good-quality red wine vinegar

SPICED PICKLED BEETROOT AND PINK ONION

4 tablespoons caster (superfine) sugar

4 tablespoons cider vinegar

2 small beetroots (beets), neatly peeled and very finely sliced (use a vegetable peeler)

½ red onion, finely sliced

1 bay leaf

2 star anise

pinch of sea salt

3 black peppercorns

small thumb-sized piece of fresh ginger, peeled

TO SERVE

4 crusty French or sourdough baguettes

sliced Gruyère or Cheddar (optional)

good-quality potato crisps (chips) (optional)

> Preheat the oven to 160°C (350°F/Gas 4).

> Season the oxtail pieces generously with salt, pepper and the garlic granules. Heat the oil in a heavy-based ovenproof casserole and fry the oxtail pieces for about 3 minutes on each side until browned. Transfer the meat to a plate and wipe any excess oil from the pan with kitchen paper. Add the olive oil and sauté the onion for 4–5 minutes, until soft and translucent. Add the carrots, celery and bay leaves and cook for a further 5–7 minutes, until aromatic and starting to colour slightly. Pour in the red wine and scrape any crust up from the bottom of the pan – this is where the flavour is! Return the oxtail to the casserole, along with the star anise, and cover the meat

with the chicken stock. Give it a stir, cover with a lid or foil, and put it in the oven to braise for 3–3½ hours, until the meat is falling off the bone.

> While the oxtail is in the oven, make the pickles. Sterilise a jar by putting it through a hot dishwasher cycle or washing it in hot, soapy water, rinsing well and drying it in a hot oven for 10 minutes. Stir the sugar and vinegar together in a mixing bowl until the sugar has dissolved. Add the beetroot and onion slices and stir to coat. Transfer to a non-stick pan and add the bay leaf, star anise, salt, peppercorns, ginger and 1 tablespoon of water. Bring to the boil and simmer for a minute or so. Transfer to the sterilised jar, leave the lid off until cooled, and then seal. »»➤

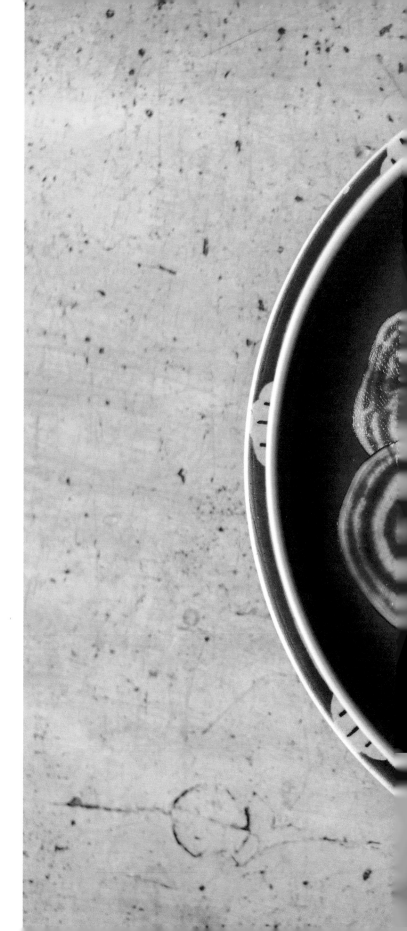

> Once cooked, remove the oxtail from the casserole with a slotted spoon and allow to cool slightly (leave the oven on). Shred the meat from the bone into a separate bowl, and discard the bones. Pass the braising liquor through a fine sieve into a glass jug and skim off as much fat as you can from the surface. Return the liquor to the casserole and reduce over a medium heat for about 5 minutes.

> Heat some little bowls for the gravy in the oven.

> Mix the butter and flour together until you have a smooth paste (*roux*), and add it to the braising liquor over the heat, using a whisk to incorporate it (this will begin to thicken the sauce as it cooks). Cook for another 10 minutes for the flour to cook out and the sauce to turn into a thick-ish gravy. Taste for seasoning, and add 1 teaspoon or so of red wine vinegar for acidity. Turn the heat down to its lowest setting and keep the gravy warm.

> Just before serving, immerse the oxtail in the warm gravy over the heat for a couple of minutes to warm it through, before removing it with a slotted spoon.

> Slice open the baguettes, and fill with the gravy-coated oxtail. Top with the pickles and Gruyère or Cheddar, and serve with little bowls of the hot gravy. Dip and enjoy! Alternatively, if you don't mind things getting messy, just pour the gravy all over your sandwich. Serve with some potato crisps.

Bavette + chips with bottarga butter + grilled baby gem

*W*ho doesn't love steak and chips? When I really fancy a steak – perhaps for a cosy night in – I usually go for bavette. In the UK, this cheaper cut, known as a 'butcher's cut' because it's so flavoursome the butchers keep it back for themselves, is also known as skirt steak. It comes from the flank of the animal, and boasts amazing succulence and tenderness. Here I've paired it with my ultimate umami butter, made with bottarga, the dried roe of the grey mullet. This Italian delicacy doesn't come cheap – so you'll be pleased that you saved on the steak – but it's worth investing in every once in a while because the amber roe is so intense and delicious it adds an incredible savoury richness, and it keeps for ages. When mixed into butter it's like the most wonderful intense anchovy butter you've ever tasted, and what you don't use you can freeze and save for another time, to smother on pasta or cooked greens. If you can't find bottarga, use best-quality anchovy fillets.

---

500 g (1 lb 2 oz) bavette steak

20 g (¾ oz) bottarga (or 8 best-quality anchovy fillets, minced)

50 g (2 oz) unsalted butter, softened, plus extra for the sauce

grated zest and juice of ½ unwaxed lemon

4 medium white potatoes, peeled and cut into chips (fries)

800 ml (30 fl oz) vegetable, sunflower or groundnut oil

3 sprigs rosemary, leaves picked and roughly chopped

sea salt and freshly ground black pepper

olive oil, for greasing

1 head of baby gem lettuce, cleaned and cut in half

50 ml (2 fl oz) chicken stock or water

> Take the steak out of the fridge 30 minutes before you cook it, to bring it up to room temperature.

> To make the bottarga butter, finely grate the bottarga into a bowl, add the 50 g (2 oz) of butter and lemon zest, and mash together thoroughly. Place 2 layers of cling film (plastic wrap) on a work surface, spoon the butter into the middle of it, and tightly roll, twisting the ends, so you have a cling film-coated sausage of butter. Place in the freezer to set.

> To make the chips, dry the potato pieces with kitchen paper, and, if using a deep-fat fryer, heat the oil to 190°C (375°F/Gas 5). Fry the chips in two batches for 7–10 minutes, until golden brown and soft on the inside. Drain them on kitchen paper and toss with fresh rosemary and sea salt. Lay on a roasting tray and keep in a warmed oven (100°C/215°F/Gas ½) until you're ready to dish up, blasting them on a really high heat for a few minutes just before you serve. If you don't have a deep-fat fryer, toss the chips with plenty of olive oil, salt and rosemary, and roast them in one layer in a preheated oven at 180°C (350°F/Gas 4) for 35–40 minutes, turning them halfway through, until crisp and golden on the ouside and soft and fluffy on the inside.

> Season the steak thoroughly with salt and pepper on both sides. Heat a greased heavy-based frying pan (skillet) until stinking hot. Put the steak in the pan (it should sizzle immediately) and cook for 3–5 minutes on each side for medium-rare or 5–7 minutes for well done. Transfer to a chopping board (but keep the steak pan), cover loosely with foil and leave to rest. Remove the bottarga butter from the freezer and put two plates in the oven to warm.

> Brush the cut sides of the baby gem halves with olive oil and place them face down in the steak pan, over a medium heat. Leave for 2 minutes then pour over the chicken stock or water to deglaze, add a knob of butter, and pour over the lemon juice. Sauté for 3–4 minutes, until wilted and caramelised on the cut side but still retaining their shape.

> Slice the rested steak into thin slivers, against the grain, and divide between the warmed plates along with any juices that might have escaped. Cut the end off the bottarga butter sausage and cut 2 x 5 mm (¼ in) thick rounds of the butter for each steak, making sure to peel the cling film (plastic wrap) off the outside edges. Place the butter directly onto the steak and serve with the chips and baby gem. Note: If you want your bottarga butter to melt, just flash the plates under a hot grill for a minute or two.

Cuts like the BAVETTE or OXTAIL are cheaper + yield AMAZING flavours; they should be celebrated not disregarded.

James Lowe's cod cheeks with green sauce + potatoes

M y friend James is a fantastic chef. In the absurdly stressful run-up to opening his first restaurant, Lyle's in Shoreditch, he managed to spare an afternoon to teach me this dish in my tiny kitchen. I will always thank him for that. The dish centres around wonderful thrifty and meaty cod cheeks, which you'll probably need to ask your fishmonger for a couple of days in advance. It's a brilliant dish for its simplicity, purity and vibrancy, and it's also a masterclass in balancing flavours. Have a go, and, as James would say, remember to use your palate to guide you when you're cooking. James is very particular about ingredients. He says 'Life's too short for bad vinegar, oil and anchovies' and advises using the best possible quality you can find to make this dish really special. I'm not about to argue!

---

300 g (10½ oz) small new potatoes (ideally Jersey Royals or Yukon Golds), washed

5 g (¼ oz) wakame seaweed (available from health-food stores and Asian grocery stores)

sea salt

500 g (1 lb 2 oz) cod cheeks, cleaned and sinew removed (if you can't find cod cheeks, fillets of any firm white fish like cod, coley or pollock will do)

flavourless oil (rapeseed, groundnut or sunflower oil)

juice of ½ lemon

GREEN SAUCE

80 ml (2½ fl oz) extra-virgin olive oil

15 g (½ oz) tarragon leaves

15 g (½ oz) flat-leaf parsley leaves

1 garlic clove

1 teaspoon Dijon mustard

10 g (½ oz) small capers, rinsed

20 g (¾ oz) good-quality salt-packed anchovies, rinsed and chopped

generous pinch of sea salt

1–2 tablespoons good-quality cider vinegar with mother (or other good-quality vinegar)

> Put the potatoes in a medium saucepan and cover them with water until there's about 2 cm (1 in) of water above the surface of the potatoes. Add the seaweed, cover and bring to a simmer. Turn the heat down slightly and taste the water for salt. You want it salty but not overly so, as you'll use some of this stock for the sauce: add salt accordingly. Simmer the potatoes for 15–20 minutes until they're cooked and you can easily slide a knife or fork into them. Once they're cooked, leave them standing in the cooking water off the heat while you prepare the rest of the dish – it will intensify their earthy potato flavour.

> Now make the green sauce. If you're making it in a food processor, pour in the olive oil, then add the herbs, garlic and Dijon mustard, blitz and transfer to a mixing bowl.

If you're making it by hand, chop the herbs finely and put them in a mixing bowl with the oil, garlic and Dijon mustard and combine thoroughly.

> Add the capers, 7 g (¼ oz) of the anchovies and the sea salt. Stir well and taste it – it should be grassy and green, but in need of a lift. Begin to add the vinegar, a little at a time, stirring vigorously and tasting as you go. You want the vinegar to pique the sauce with its acidity and bring out its fresh punch. James says: 'This is the main acidic element to the dish and it will be used to heighten the rest of the food, so acidify with the vinegar until it almost makes you salivate! In a good way.' Vinegars vary in acidity depending on quality, so you need to trust your palate here and add as much as you think it needs. >>>➤

> Heat a heavy-based frying pan (skillet) over a high heat until it's stinking hot. Season the cod cheeks on one side with sea salt. Drizzle a dash of oil into the pan to coat the surface and add the cheeks, salty side down. Leave them untouched and let them cook for 1–2 minutes until they form a nice golden crust and come away easily from the bottom of the pan. Once they have coloured, flip them over and cook them for another 2 minutes (cook them for no longer than 5 minutes in total). Remove any smaller cod cheeks from the pan while you make the sauce as they will cook much quicker. Turn the heat down slightly and add the lemon juice. Then add 3 tablespoons of the potato stock, and swirl it around the pan to deglaze, being sure to scrape up any bits from the bottom of the pan – this is where the flavour is. Drain and add the potatoes, remaining anchovies and any cod cheeks you may have removed, to warm through.

> To serve, plate up 3–4 potatoes per person along with pieces of seaweed, and divide the cheeks between the plates. Pour over the pan sauce and drizzle the green sauce on top. Enjoy!

> **TIP:** James has a brilliant tip for making any kind of fresh sauce with chopped herbs, whether you're making it in a food processor or in a bowl with hand-cut herbs: always start with olive oil. It coats the chopped herbs and stops them from oxidising, keeping them brighter and fresher for longer.

Pan-roasted pollock with lettuce, bacon + clams

This is my version of a restaurant dish I've had in various guises, and would always order if it was on the menu. I love the combination of meaty, flaky white fish with a slightly golden crust, cooked with delicate sweet clams and wilted, but still-crunchy lettuce. I've used pollock because it's cheaper and more plentiful than cod, and, in my opinion, just as tasty, but you could use cod, coley, hake or haddock. Cooked lettuce is a favourite of mine – I love what applying heat does to its texture, making it silky while retaining a subtle fresh flavour and satisfying bite. I've used home-made fish stock to give the sauce depth and refinement – it's well worth making if you have time. All the work here is in what chefs call the 'mise en place' – the preparation – and is ideal for a romantic evening in or dinner party, as, once you've done the prep, it all comes together quickly, leaving you time to have your fun.

2 thick pollock or hake fillets or other white fish (ask the fishmonger to remove the skin)

sea salt and freshly ground black pepper

large handful of clams or cockles, in their shells, cleaned

light olive oil

unsalted butter

2 shallots, finely sliced

1 garlic clove, crushed

1 bay leaf

2 rashers (slices) of smoked back bacon, cut into lardons, or 50 g (2 oz) good-quality lardons

100 ml (3½ fl oz) white wine

300 ml (10 fl oz) fish stock (preferably home-made, see page 238, but a cube is fine)

2 tablespoons double (heavy) cream

1 tablespoon freshly squeezed lemon juice

1 sprig thyme, leaves picked

8 leaves of baby gem or romaine lettuce, washed and sliced

1 tablespoon finely chopped flat-leaf parsley leaves

> Season the fish fillets with a little sea salt 2 hours before cooking – this will help to draw out excess water. Keep the clams or cockles in a bowl in the fridge with a damp tea towel over them. Before cooking, place the clams or cockles in a bowl of water under a gently running cold tap for about 10 minutes – this will encourage them to give up their grit.

> Heat a dessertspoonful of olive oil and a knob of butter in a pan. Add the shallots, garlic and bay leaf, and cook for 2 minutes over a medium heat, until they're starting to soften. Add the lardons and cook for a further 5 minutes, stirring to coat the shallots in the bacon fat. Add the white wine and reduce until it's mostly evaporated, then add the fish stock and reduce again by almost half (another 8–10 minutes). Add the cream, bring back to the boil and simmer for 2 more minutes. Take off the heat, remove the bay and season with lemon juice. Taste the sauce to make sure it's to your liking, and add more salt, lemon or cream to your taste.

> Heat a little bit of oil in a heavy-based frying pan (skillet) until stinking hot, and add the seasoned pollock fillets. Cook for about 4 minutes, until they've formed a nice golden brown crust and come away from the pan easily, then flip them over. Add a knob of butter and some thyme leaves, and cook for another 3–4 minutes. When they're cooked all the way through, and firm to the touch, transfer to a warm plate and leave to rest under some foil while you cook the clams or cockles.

> Heat a little bit more oil in the fish pan and add the drained clams or cockles and the lettuce. Put a clear lid over the pan and shake it around a bit, until the clams start to open (about 3 minutes). Transfer the contents of the pan to the shallots, bacon and stock and heat the whole thing up until it's just boiling, simmering for 1 minute, then stir in the parsley and taste for seasoning. Discard any clams that are still closed.

> Plate-up the pollock fillets then divide the clam and lettuce sauce between the two plates or bowls. I find it pays to set the table with a spoon when you make this dish, because the sauce is so delicious, you'll want to eat every last drop. It's nice served with some buttery potato purée or better still, chips!

Leek, smoked mackerel + toasted almond risotto

I always like to have a risotto rice in the cupboard as it can be a total lifesaver for a quick, warming and satisfying meal. This is an affordable and relatively simple supper that packs a real flavour punch and can be made with ingredients you won't have to travel far and wide for. I love the subtle, sweet allium flavour of the leeks, and the nutty crunch of the toasted almonds adds texture to this silky, creamy dish. When making risotto, it's important to keep stirring the rice as you cook it, to release its starch and make the dish really creamy. If you've made the Preserved lemons on page 233, or have a jar in your fridge, a little bit sliced and fried with the leeks gives the dish a lovely citrusy note.

2 smoked mackerel fillets (I prefer plain rather than peppered ones)

juice of ½ lemon

25 g (1 oz) butter, and 1 extra knob to finish

2 slices of preserved lemon, flesh and pith removed, finely chopped (optional)

1 large leek, tough outer leaves removed, rinsed thoroughly and finely sliced

50 g (2 oz/generous ½ cup) flaked almonds

220 g (8 oz/1 cup) arborio risotto rice

120 ml (4 fl oz) dry white wine (pinot grigio is better for risotto than to drink)

1 litre (34 fl oz) warm chicken or fish stock (preferably home-made, see page 236 or 238, but a cube is fine)

2 tablespoons freshly grated Parmesan

sea salt and freshly ground black pepper

rocket (arugula) leaves or watercress, to serve

> Remove the skin from the mackerel fillets and flake them into a dish. Add the lemon juice. Melt the butter in a large non-stick frying pan (skillet) or heavy-based saucepan over a medium heat and add the preserved lemon (if using) and sliced leek. Sauté, gently stirring for about 5 minutes, or until softened and fragrant. While you're doing this, toast the flaked almonds in a dry frying pan (skillet) over a medium heat until golden brown, being careful not to burn them. Remove from heat and set aside.

> Add the rice to the leeks and coat in the butter, stirring over the heat for a couple of minutes until the rice turns translucent. Pour in the white wine, stirring, and once most of the wine has evaporated add the stock, a ladleful at a time, stirring frequently and waiting for most of the stock to be absorbed before adding the next ladleful. Repeat this process a ladleful at a time, for 20–30 minutes, until all the stock is absorbed, and the rice is plump and creamy but still a little al dente, retaining a little bite, but with no hard chalky core. Take off the heat, add a knob of butter, the Parmesan, flaked mackerel and lemon juice, and stir gently to combine. Season to taste, garnish with the toasted almonds and serve with rocket leaves or watercress.

SERVES
**2 as a main,
4 as a pasta course**

Nduja + squid ink vongole

Nduja is one of my most treasured ingredients. It was first given to me by the Calabrian chef Francesco Mazzei, who introduced Londoners to the powerful, spicy flavours of Southern Italian cooking when he opened his brilliant restaurant L'Anima in the City. Nduja is a soft, spreadable, incredibly spicy Calabrian cured pork sausage that brings an instant hot, savoury depth to any dish. Here it adds oomph to my favourite Italian pasta dish of spaghetti vongole. I love the way it contrasts with the sweet, juicy clams, and seasons the dish with fiery chillies. I've used Squid ink spaghetti (see page 134) because I'm a sucker for its added umami and dramatic darkness, but you could also use plain spaghetti or store-bought squid ink pasta. If you've made bottarga butter for the steak recipe on page 118, you could stir a knob of it through the pasta before serving for some extra boom!

**400 g (14 oz) clams,
cleaned**

**2 tablespoons extra-virgin
olive oil**

**1 banana shallot, finely
chopped**

**1 large garlic clove,
crushed**

**50 g (2 oz) nduja, coating
discarded**

**1 portion of Squid ink
spaghetti, shop-bought or
home-made (see page 134)**

**50 ml (2 fl oz) dry
white wine**

**30 g (1 oz) flat-leaf parsley,
stems and leaves, washed
and finely chopped**

**grated zest and juice of
½ unwaxed lemon**

sea salt

**knob of bottarga butter
(see page 118) (optional)**

➤ Keep your clams in a bowl in the fridge with a damp tea towel over them. Before cooking, place the clams in a bowl of water under a gently running cold tap for about 10 minutes – this will encourage them to give up their grit.

➤ Bring a large saucepan of very salty water to the boil. Heat 1 tablespoon of the olive oil in a heavy-based frying pan (skillet) and fry the shallot and garlic for a couple of minutes, until softened. Add the nduja and cook, stirring, until it breaks down and melts into the shallot base, turning it red. Remove from the heat.

➤ Cook the pasta in the boiling water until al dente. If you're using home-made squid ink spaghetti this will only take 2 minutes. Drain, reserving about 1 tablespoon of the cooking water.

➤ Return the nduja and shallot to the heat. Add the drained clams and white wine, and shake the pan to combine all the ingredients. Cover with a lid and cook for a few minutes, until the clams have opened (discard any that are still closed) and the alcohol has cooked out. Add the cooked pasta, parsley and the tablespoon of cooking water to the frying pan and toss everything together, so the pasta is cooked in the glossy emulsion. Remove from the heat and transfer to a large bowl. Season with lemon juice and zest, drizzle with the remaining olive oil (or stir through the bottarga butter, if using), and serve, along with a bowl for the shells.

Kale + almond pesto linguine

A bag of kale can go a long way. It doesn't wither in the fridge like spinach or broccoli, you can steam it, roast it into wonderfully crisp chips (see page 105), sauté it in a little bit of olive oil, use it to bulk-out and health-up various soups, stews and salads, and, as I do here, make it into a tasty pesto to slather on linguine. It's delicious, super-simple to whizz up, economical, and will completely negate any guilt you might feel (you shouldn't) about eating a big old bowl of pasta...

3 spring onions (scallions), trimmed and roughly chopped

4 garlic cloves, peeled but left whole

80 g (3 oz) curly kale, stems removed and washed

40 g (1½ oz/scant ½ cup) flaked almonds

4 tablespoons extra-virgin olive oil, plus extra for covering the pesto

35 g (1¼ oz) flat-leaf parsley leaves

35 g (1¼ oz) basil leaves

generous pinch of red chilli flakes

grated zest of ½ unwaxed lemon, and 1 tablespoon freshly squeezed lemon juice

25 g (1 oz) grated Parmesan, plus extra to serve

sea salt and freshly ground black pepper

75 g (2½ oz) linguine per person

› Sterilise a jar by putting it through a hot dishwasher cycle or washing it in hot, soapy water, rinsing well and drying it in a hot oven for 10 minutes.

› Bring a large pan of salted water to the boil. Add the spring onions and garlic and cook for 3 minutes, until they're soft. Add the kale and cook for no more than 40 seconds, until it's bright green and floppy. Don't overcook it as it will lose that lovely bright green colour.

› Lift out the kale with a slotted spoon and put it onto a plate. Lift out the garlic and spring onion (don't discard the cooking water) and blitz them in a food processor with the almonds. Add the olive oil, parsley, basil, chilli flakes and blitz again. Squeeze the excess water out of the kale and add it to the food processor too, blitzing, followed by the lemon juice and zest, and Parmesan. Season with black pepper and salt to taste, and stir. Store the pesto in the sterilised jar, covering it with a layer of olive oil to seal in the freshness.

› Cook the linguine in the same water that you blanched the kale in for about 6–7 minutes, or until al dente. Drain, reserving a splash of the pasta water, return to the pan and stir in generous tablespoons of the pesto and the reserved pasta water, and season with freshly ground black pepper and more Parmesan.

SERVES
2 as a main or
4 as a starter

Squid ink pasta

I've had a thing for squid and cuttlefish ink ever since I first ate black risotto in Italy many years ago. I love the unrelenting blackness of it, and the umami it adds to dishes. Mixing it into pasta dough makes for the most beautiful jet-black pasta with a hint of the sea, just great for seafood or pork-based pasta dishes.

200 g (7 oz/1⅔ cups) '00' pasta flour (superfine '00' grade), plus extra for dusting

pinch of sea salt

2 eggs

5 g (¼ oz) squid ink (available from most fishmongers)

semolina flour, for dusting

SPECIAL EQUIPMENT

pasta machine

› Fill a small bowl with water and dust a work surface with flour. Sift the flour into a large mixing bowl and make a well in the centre with your fingers. Scatter the salt onto the flour and crack the eggs into the well, adding the squid ink too. Using the blade of a table knife, break up the egg yolks and, working outwards in a circular motion, start to draw in and incorporate the flour, using the side of the knife blade to mix it all together until you have clumps. Use your fingers to bring it together into a ball, squidging it against any smaller crumbs to incorporate them.

› Once you have a ball of dough, turn it, and any remaining flour, onto the floured work surface. Wet your fingers slightly and start to knead the dough, pressing and stretching it with the ball of your hand. Work the dough for 5–10 minutes, until it's smooth, soft, uniformly black and springs back into form when squashed. Cut the dough in half to make 2 balls and wrap each in cling film (plastic wrap). Keep chilled for 1 hour.

› Once rested, remove the pasta dough from the cling film and place one of the pasta balls on a floured surface. Press it down with the palm of your hand and roll it out with a floured rolling pin, so that it's thin enough to fit through the thickest setting on the pasta machine and the same width as the pasta machine. Pass the dough through the rollers of the machine on its thickest setting a couple of times then continue to run it through the pasta machine, gradually reducing the settings to 2 below the thinnest setting. Run it through this setting a couple more times, until it's a thin sheet, about the width of spaghetti. You don't want to run it through the machine more than 8 times. Lay the sheet of pasta out on the work surface and roll out the other ball of pasta.

› Once all the dough is rolled, and both sheets are on the work surface (each one should be 30–40 cm/12–16 in long), cut each piece in half, so that it's 15–20 cm (6–8 in) long. Now, using a spaghetti attachment for your pasta machine, run it through once to make spaghetti. Repeat with the other sheets. Lay your spaghetti on a flat baking sheet, sprinkle with semolina flour and chill for at least 3 hours to dry it out before cooking. See the recipe for Nduja and squid ink pasta on page 131 for cooking instructions.

› **NOTE:** If you don't have a spaghetti attachment, fold your sheets in half and use a sharp knife to cut them into fettuccine-width strips

Uyen Luu's crispy sea bream fillets with rice noodles + sweetheart cabbage

My friend Uyen Luu is a Vietnamese supper club hostess, food writer, stylist and excellent cook, and she always says the key to Vietnamese food is 'to get the right balance of sweet, sour, salty and hot'. She turned me on to using Vietnamese fish sauce (nuoc mam) in my cooking, and now I find myself adding it to things like spag bol, marinades and stocks for extra savoury depth. At her supper club, Uyen serves a mixture of traditional and contemporary Vietnamese dishes. This is one of her more modern creations and I love it because, like lots of Vietnamese food, it elevates quite humble ingredients into something really special thanks to its well-pitched contrast of sweet, salty, sour and spicy. Uyen says, 'Prep all the ingredients for this recipe beforehand as it's fast work over the stove.'

SAUCE

3 tablespoons good-quality fish sauce (Uyen favours the Three Crabs brand)

1 bird's-eye chilli, chopped

1 tablespoon honey

1 teaspoon chilli oil

juice of ½ lime

2 tablespoons flavourless oil (rapeseed, groundnut or sunflower)

400 g (14 oz) or 2 fillets of sea bream, skin-on, scaled

200 g (7 oz) dried flat rice noodles

25 g (1 oz) shallot, sliced

120 g (4 oz) sweetheart cabbage, washed and sliced into thin 1 cm (½ in) ribbons

2 spring onions (scallions), finely sliced

10 g (½ oz) coriander (cilantro) leaves or mint, sliced

10 g (½ oz) Thai basil (optional)

> In a bowl mix together the ingredients for the sauce.

> Heat the oil in a frying pan (skillet) over a medium heat and fry the sea bream, skin-side down, for 3–5 minutes on each side, until the skin is crisp and the fish is cooked through. Remove from the pan and cover to keep warm.

> Place the noodles in a heatproof container, cover with boiling water and leave for 5 minutes with a lid on. Test to make sure they are al dente, drain and rinse with cold water until the starch is removed and the water runs clear.

> Using the same pan and oil that you cooked the fish in, add the shallots and cook for 2 minutes. Add the sliced cabbage, spring onions and the noodles, and fry for a further 2 minutes, stirring constantly until the cabbage leaves wilt. Pour the sauce over the noodles and toss to coat them well. Add the coriander and Thai basil (if using), fry for a further 2 minutes and remove from the heat. Divide the noodles between two serving plates, top with the fish and eat immediately.

Rosemary-fried mackerel fillets with buttered new potatoes, pickled samphire + radishes

I love fresh mackerel, and my most vivid memory of eating it was one summer in Norway when we pulled dozens of the shiny silver beauties out of the fjord with drop lines. We gutted them on the boat, cooked them as soon as we got home, fried in butter and herbs from the garden, and ate them with a pickled cucumber salad. I love how woody, aromatic rosemary works with the bold flavour of mackerel, and I've added pickled samphire for juiciness and acidity, to cut through its richness.

300 g (10½ oz) small new or Jersey Royal potatoes, washed

unsalted butter

1 tablespoon chopped chives

sea salt and freshly ground black pepper

4 fresh mackerel fillets, pin-boned

olive oil

2 sprigs rosemary

½ lemon, for juicing

small bunch of radishes (I like the colourful heirloom varieties), leaves removed, washed and very finely sliced with a mandoline

SAMPHIRE PICKLE

4 tablespoons caster (superfine) sugar

pinch of salt

4 tablespoons rice wine vinegar

100 g (3½ oz) samphire, washed

➤ Cook the potatoes in boiling, salted water for 25–30 minutes until they're soft and you can easily slide a knife or fork into them. Drain the potatoes and put them back into the pan with a knob of butter and the chives, and season with salt and pepper. Toss to coat.

➤ Now make the samphire pickle: you want to do this as close to cooking the mackerel as possible as the samphire will discolour. Dissolve the sugar and salt in the vinegar and then pour it into a saucepan along with the samphire and bring to the boil. Remove from the heat, and transfer to a bowl, letting the samphire steep in the pickle juice and turning it over occasionally with your hands to coat.

➤ Season the mackerel fillets with a little salt and pepper. Heat a little olive oil in a heavy-based frying pan (skillet), add the rosemary and stir into the oil, then cook the mackerel for 2–3 minutes, skin-side down, pressing it down with a fish slice, until the skin is crisp. Flip them over, add a knob of butter, and cook for another 2 minutes, until the flesh is opaque, basting the fish with the herb-infused butter as you go. To serve, lay the potatoes out on a platter, surrounded by the samphire pickle, and arrange the fillets on top. Scatter over the sliced radish, squeeze over some lemon juice and enjoy.

CHAPTER 5

Feasts for friends

I'M A FEEDER. IT'S IN MY BLOOD.

Mum is the same, and still, whenever I return to the warmth of her house, she starts offering me something to eat the minute I get through the door. If she had her way I'd be eating sandwiches and drinking wine in the middle of the afternoon, for no particular reason (not that there's anything wrong with that).

I remember being a child and marvelling at the dinner parties my parents used to host for their friends and our extended family. I used to creep around in my pyjamas, unable to sleep, peering curiously into the dining room to see trolleys of drinks, wooden boards oozing with cheese, and the glitter from candlesticks on the dining table, half-empty wine bottles and plates piled with food. Occasionally I was roped in to help, and I was the most eager of waitresses when it came to dishing out canapés to my parents' guests – it was my way of getting in on the action and sneaking mouthfuls when no-one was looking. These dinner parties always felt like an exclusive, alluring adult world of enchantment, and I longed for the days when I would be old enough to sip from a cut crystal glass and eat vol-au-vents.

Of course, by the time I was old enough to host my own dinner parties and lavish my pals with food, all of this formality had become terribly passé. If I folded napkins into lily flowers and handed out devilled egg mayonnaise in pastry cases everyone would assume I was hosting an *Abigail's Party*-themed dinner (which I fully intend on doing some time). We live in an age where a dinner party is just that – a real party – and I

think food for entertaining should reflect this, so you can serve cocktails in jam jars (no one will cry if they get smashed), and pile platters into the middle of the table so folks can help themselves and pass them along. If you're anything like me, you'll want to keep it relaxed so that you can get on with the important stuff like drinking and dancing with your mates. And who the room for a 'dinner set' these days?

While throwing a dinner party or cooking for friends should be all about generosity, deliciousness and abundance, it shouldn't cost the earth, so in this chapter you'll find ideas for feasts which don't rely on expensive produce to please your pals. 'Wow' dishes like the Home-style porchetta (see page 154) or Maple-braised pig's cheeks (see page 149) might require a bit of time in terms of prep, but can then be left to slow cook while you get everything else ready, and are guaranteed to put a big smile on your guests' faces – they've certainly gone down well at my supper clubs.

Then there are faster options like the smoky sweet Chipotle roast chicken (see page 163), which can be torn up at the table and loaded onto tortillas, while you tear into the margaritas. Break-up lasagne with radicchio, walnuts and dreamy Gorgonzola béchamel (see page 146) is bound to perk up even those with aching hearts, and can easily be made ahead, while top Indian chef Vivek Singh's Killer vegetable curry (see page 169) is the perfect fridge and store-cupboard dish to have in your arsenal for when guests pop over unexpectedly. All of these dishes are designed to serve generous portions to feed people who are as greedy as me.

Chicken, mushroom + tarragon cassoulet

I came up with this recipe while my boyfriend and I were on a road trip down the West Coast of the US. We'd driven from Oregon to California in relentless torrential rain and were hungry when we got to Eureka. The weather had put a bit of a dampener on the trip, but thankfully the first grocery store we stopped at had some wonderful chanterelles and corn-fed chicken, so I busied myself making up a comforting recipe for a rainy summer's day in our tiny rented studio flat. We ate it with a bottle of fantastic Californian zinfandel, and ended up feeling thankful for our rainy night in.

3 medium tomatoes, sliced, or 1 large handful of cherry tomatoes, halved

extra-virgin olive oil

sea salt and freshly ground black pepper

25 g (1 oz) butter

1 garlic clove, crushed

3 small shallots, finely chopped

handful of fresh tarragon, roughly chopped, plus extra to garnish

100 g (3½ oz) chanterelles, little ones whole and bigger ones broken up

2 large portobello mushrooms, cleaned gently with kitchen paper if necessary, sliced

50 g (2 oz) chestnut or button mushrooms, cleaned gently with kitchen paper if necessary, halved

bunch of flat-leaf parsley, leaves, finely chopped

1–2 teaspoons white wine or tarragon vinegar

8 free-range chicken thighs, skin on

150 ml (5 fl oz) white wine

80 g (3 oz) kalamata olives, pitted and sliced

500–700 ml (17–24 fl oz) chicken stock or water

400 g (14 oz) tin cannellini beans, drained and rinsed

> Preheat the oven to 180°C (350°F/Gas 4). Place the tomatoes in a roasting tray, coat them in 1 tablespoon of olive oil, and season with salt and pepper. Roast for 15–20 minutes, until they're concentrated and aromatic. While they're roasting, heat a large heavy-based frying pan (skillet) or ovenproof casserole, add the butter, garlic and half the chopped shallots, and cook for about 2 minutes, until they start to soften. Add the tarragon, mushrooms, a pinch of salt and a grind of pepper. Sauté for about 5 minutes, until the mushrooms are tinged golden brown, and have started to release their moisture and crisp around the edges. Depending on the size of your frying pan, you may have to work in batches. Transfer to a bowl, and remove the tomatoes from the oven.

> Stir the chopped parsley and 1 teaspoon of vinegar into the mushrooms, and taste for seasoning/acidity. You want to bring out the mushrooms' flavour, not mask it, so add a dash more vinegar if you think it needs it.

> Heat another tablespoon of olive oil in the frying pan you cooked the mushrooms in, over a medium-high heat. Add the chicken thighs, skin-side down, and fry until golden, turning them once or twice to brown them evenly. The skin should be crispy on each side. Transfer to a plate. Add the remaining shallots to the pan and fry for 4 minutes, until soft.

> Deglaze the pan with the white wine so that it picks up the crusty goodness from browning the chicken, and place the chicken back in the pan, along with the olives. Pour in the water or stock until it's covering the chicken and bring to the boil. Turn down the heat and simmer for 35 minutes.

> Add the roasted tomatoes and stir, then add the beans. Bring back to a boil, then turn down to a simmer. After 5 minutes add the mushrooms and shallots, and simmer for 7–10 minutes, until the sauce has reduced and gone a bit creamy from the beans. Garnish with tarragon leaves and serve with a crisp, sharply-dressed salad and crusty bread for dunking.

Radicchio, Gorgonzola + walnut break-up lasagne

Despite being meat-free, this vegetarian lasagne is serious comfort food. I fed it to one of my closest friends on the night of her break-up and it seemed to work wonders for her battered spirit, along with a few generous glasses of red wine. Bitter radicchio and creamy, salty Gorgonzola are often found together with walnuts in a salad and they really harmonise into something special when cooked together. You can make a wonderful meaty version by replacing the wilted radicchio with speck or prosciutto, or a pork and beef ragu, but this one's for the veggies. Pair it with a simple salad of peppery leaves and tomatoes dressed with good-quality olive oil and red wine vinegar.

50 g (2 oz) unsalted butter, plus extra for greasing

40 g (1½ oz/⅓ cup) plain (all-purpose) flour

600 ml (20 fl oz) whole milk

nutmeg, for grating

200 g (7 oz) Gorgonzola, diced

sea salt and freshly ground black pepper

extra-virgin olive oil

leaves from 2 large heads of radicchio, hard white cores removed, washed and dried (500 g/1 lb 2 oz)

1 tablespoon freshly squeezed lemon juice

handful of flat-leaf parsley leaves, finely chopped

80 g (3 oz) walnuts, crumbled slightly

dried lasagne egg pasta

150 g (5 oz) mozzarella, grated

20 g (¾ oz) Parmesan, grated

> Preheat the oven to 180°C (350°F/Gas 4) and grease a large baking dish. Melt the butter in a non-stick saucepan over a medium heat, then add the flour and cook, stirring, for a minute or so, until the roux is starting to bubble. Turn the heat down and add the milk, a little at a time, stirring constantly until it's amalgamated and smooth. Use a whisk to whisk out any lumps. Once you have a smooth sauce, cook it for about 10 minutes, whisking while it thickens. Add a good grating of nutmeg, a generous grind of black pepper and then add the Gorgonzola. Melt it over the heat for a couple of minutes, whisking, until you have a smooth, creamy béchamel. Season with salt and pepper. Set aside.

> Heat 1 tablespoon of olive oil in a heavy-based frying pan (skillet) and add the radicchio leaves (depending on the size of your pan, you may need to work in batches). Grind over some pepper, add the lemon juice, and cook it for 3–4 minutes, until slightly wilted. Transfer to a mixing bowl and toss with the parsley.

> Lay some of the wilted radicchio and parsley on the base of the greased baking dish, scatter over some of the walnuts, and top with some of the Gorgonzola béchamel. Lay pasta sheets on top until entirely covering the radicchio and repeat the process with the remaining ingredients for 2 more layers. Top the last layer of pasta with mozzarella and Parmesan, and bake in the oven for 30–40 minutes, until golden on top, and the béchamel is bubbling up the sides of the dish. Allow to rest for about 10 minutes and then serve.

Maple-braised pigs' cheeks with apple, roasted hazelnuts + Parmesan polenta

This is one of my favourite recipes from my time living in Vancouver, when maple syrup and locally-grown hazelnuts were a happy staple in my kitchen. I lived really close to a brilliant biodynamic and organic butcher who I'd pester for unusual cuts like oxtail, tongue and pigs' cheeks. You might need to ask your butcher in advance for pig's cheeks, but it's worth the extra effort as when cooked slowly in this rich braise, they are melty, yet meaty, yielding and gorgeous – just perfect with crunchy hazelnuts and tart pickled apple. I serve them with wet polenta to soak up all those maple-y juices, but it would be just as nice with gnocchi, buttery potato purée or fettuccine.

---

50 g (2 oz) skinless roasted hazelnuts

PICKLED APPLE GARNISH

1 teaspoon sea salt

1 tablespoon caster (superfine) sugar

1 teaspoon maple syrup

2 tablespoons cider vinegar

½ apple, peeled, cored and cut into small, even-sized cubes or very thinly sliced

PORK

1 kg (2 lb 3 oz) pigs' cheeks (you could also use neck, butt or shoulder steaks, cut into large slices)

sea salt and freshly ground black pepper

1–2 tablespoons olive oil

1 onion, chopped

1 carrot, diced

2 sticks celery, sliced

1 tablespoon tomato purée

2 apples, peeled, cored and cubed

2 bay leaves

4 cloves

2 star anise

1 sprig thyme, leaves picked

1 medium glass white wine

45 ml (1¾ fl oz) maple syrup

700 ml (24 fl oz) chicken or vegetable stock (preferably home-made, see page 236, but a cube is fine)

knob of unsalted butter

½ lemon, for squeezing

POLENTA

400 ml (13 fl oz) chicken stock (preferably home-made, see page 236, but a cube is fine)

generous pinch of salt

bay leaf

200 ml (7 fl oz) milk

120 g (4 oz) polenta

10 g (½ oz) butter

30 g (1 oz) Parmesan, grated

extra-virgin olive oil

sage leaves, finely chopped (optional)

> To make the apple pickle, dissolve the salt, sugar and syrup in the vinegar in a bowl and add the apple cubes or slices. Set aside.

> Preheat the oven to 160°C (320°F/Gas 3).

> Season the cheeks (other cuts may need cutting into pieces) all over with salt and pepper. Heat the oil in an ovenproof casserole, or a deep pan that can go in the oven, and brown the cheeks evenly over a medium-high heat.

> Transfer the cheeks to a plate. Using the residual oil, and a little more if you need to, turn the heat down slightly and add the onion, carrot and celery with a pinch of salt and good grind of black pepper, and cook for 8–10 minutes, until aromatic and they start to caramelise and colour slightly.

> Add the tomato purée and cook for a further minute before adding half the cubed apple, bay leaves, cloves, star anise, thyme and wine. Stir thoroughly and make sure you scrape up any bits that might have stuck to the bottom of the pan. Bring to the boil, turn the heat down and reduce for 2 minutes. Put the pork back in the pan, followed by enough stock to cover it. Bring it back to the boil, turn down to a simmer, and cover. Cook in the oven for 2–3 hours, until the meat is falling apart. »»→

> When the pork is done, keep it warm in a very low oven and cook the polenta.

> Put the chicken stock, salt, bay leaf and milk in a saucepan and bring to the boil. When it's boiling, begin to slowly, steadily pour in the polenta while gently whisking, until it's all combined. Turn the heat down to a simmer and cook, stirring with a wooden spoon occasionally, for 30 minutes, or until the polenta has absorbed all the liquid and is creamy and soft. If you're using quick-cook polenta, you will just need to stir it into the liquid and cook it over the heat for a minute, then remove it. Once cooked, stir in the butter, Parmesan and a splash of olive oil, and leave in a warm place until you're ready to serve.

> To finish the pork, remove it from the oven and, using a slotted spoon, transfer the meat carefully to a warm plate and cover with foil. Pass the braising liquid through a sieve and put the liquid back in the pan, discarding the vegetables and aromatics. Bring it to a gentle boil and simmer, reducing by about a quarter for 5 minutes. Then add the maple syrup and reduce by another quarter for a further 5–7 minutes. Taste for seasoning and finish it by whisking in the butter and adding a squeeze of lemon juice, to taste. Return the cheeks to the braise to coat them and warm them through over a gentle heat before serving.

> Divide the polenta between 4 plates, top with the pigs' cheeks and spoon over the sauce. Garnish with the roasted hazelnuts and pickled apple.

Cooking for *friends* should be all about GENEROSITY, DELICIOUSNESS + ABUNDANCE + it shouldn't cost the earth.

Home-style porchetta

I really love pig. Well, it takes one to know one doesn't it? There's just something so good about melty, succulent pork meat, and nothing on earth I enjoy quite as much as the crackling fat. One of the best incarnations of pork I've ever had was at a sandwich store in Vancouver called Meat and Bread, which specialises in roasted porchetta (a rolled Italian pork roast) with really crackly crackling. The tender porchetta is stuffed with fragrant herbs and served on soft, pillowy ciabatta with the crackling thrown in for good measure, then drizzled with more punchy salsa verde: just unbelievable! This is my version, and it's something I hope you'll love as much as I do (if you have leftovers, it's perfect cold in sandwiches).

To ensure really crackly crackling, I poach the pork belly in bicarbonate of soda and hot water first (a trick taught to me by my friend and fellow cook Uyen Luu, which guarantees great crackling) and then infuse it with herbs and spices for at least 12 hours, so you need to start preparing the dish the day before you cook it.

1.5 kg (3 lb 5 oz) bone-out pork belly, the same length as the tenderloin, and wide enough to wrap around it

1 tablespoon bicarbonate of soda

500 g (1 lb 2 oz) pork tenderloin, trimmed of sinew

SALT RUB

3 teaspoons fennel seeds

3 teaspoons coriander seeds

4 teaspoons red chilli flakes

1 tablespoon sea salt

HERB RUB

2 sprigs rosemary, leaves picked and chopped

2 tablespoons flat-leaf parsley leaves, chopped

3 sprigs thyme, leaves picked

8 sage leaves, finely chopped

2 garlic cloves, crushed

grated zest of
1 unwaxed lemon

SALSA VERDE

large bunch flat-leaf parsley

10 basil leaves

10 mint leaves

pinch of caster
(superfine) sugar

80 ml (2½ fl oz) extra-virgin olive oil

1 garlic clove

1 teaspoon Dijon mustard

3 canned anchovy fillets in oil, drained (or if using salt-packed, rinsed and chopped)

2 tablespoons small capers, rinsed and drained (or 6 large capers, chopped)

sea salt and freshly ground black pepper

good-quality cider or red wine vinegar, to taste

TO SERVE

1 portion of My favourite lentils (see page 92)

fresh ciabatta bread, sliced

> Score the skin of the pork belly with a very sharp knife in a cross-hatch pattern, being careful only to score down to just before where the skin meets the fat, rather than the fat itself. Bring a large saucepan or roasting tray of water to simmer, and add the bicarbonate of soda. Place the pork belly in the water and poach gently for 5 minutes. Remove it from the water and leave to cool to room temperature.

> While the belly is poaching, roast the spices for the salt rub. Place the fennel, coriander seeds and chilli flakes in a dry

frying pan (skillet) and toast over a high heat for 2 minutes, until they are fragrant. Watch them so they don't catch or burn, then transfer to a bowl and leave to cool.

> Once the pork belly has cooled, turn it skin-side down and stab it all over the underside with a knife – don't be shy here, this will help it absorb all that lovely seasoning.

> Grind the cooled spices and salt in a mini-chopper, spice grinder or pestle and mortar. »»➔

> Combine all the ingredients for the herb rub. Rub the tenderloin (the meat should be at room temperature) and the belly all over with the spiced salt rub. Lie the pork belly, skin-side down, on the work surface. Massage the herb rub all over the belly's underside. Place the tenderloin on top, wrapping the belly around it with the skin on the outside, and tie to secure with kitchen twine. Don't worry if the belly doesn't wrap all the way around – just make sure it's as tight and snug as you can get it. Place loin-side down in a baking tray, uncovered, and chill for at least 5 hours, (preferably 10). You want the skin to completely dry out so that it crisps up nicely when you roast it.

> To cook the pork, remove it from the fridge and leave it for at least 1 hour to come to room temperature before you cook it. Preheat the oven to 140°C (280°F/ Gas 1) and cook the pork for 4 hours, turning the tray every 30 minutes or so to ensure it cooks evenly. If the skin looks in danger of burning, cover it with foil – but only do this once it has crackled. Ten minutes before the end of the cooking time, turn the heat up to 200°C (400°F/ Gas 6) and roast to crackle the skin to a gorgeous golden brown (cover any bits of skin that look like they're likely to burn with foil).

> To make the salsa verde, combine the herbs, sugar, olive oil, garlic and mustard, and blitz in a food processor until you have a sauce. Transfer to a mixing bowl and stir in the anchovies, capers, and season with salt and pepper (add salt judiciously: the anchovies are salty so it may not need more). Add the vinegar little by little, a tablespoon at a time, tasting as you go, until you've piqued the sauce with acidity. This is the only acidic element in the dish, so it needs to be punchy without losing the grassy, fresh quality of the herbs. Trust your palate and judgement and taste as you go. You want the sauce to make you salivate 'in a good way'.

> Once the pork has cooked, remove it from the oven and leave it to rest for at least 30 minutes.

> When you're ready to carve, get a big chopping board. Remove the twine from the pork. Take a knife and gently trace the blade underneath the crackled skin, removing it from the fatty bottom of the belly. Cut the meat into slices with a very sharp carving knife; it should fall into nice herby slivers. Place the crackling on the board and use a big knife to chop it up into bite-sized chunks. Pile the sliced pork onto fresh ciabatta and serve with lentils and a good handful of crackling. Drizzle with salsa verde.

Lamb neck osso buco with pearl barley + squash risotto

amb neck is a relatively inexpensive cut, but boy does it pack a flavour punch. It's fatty (read flavourful), meaty and, being on the bone, takes well to being slowly cooked: the marrow melds with the other ingredients and the bones make their own stock. I suppose this is a sort of frugal osso buco – that wonderful Italian dish of veal shank and Milanese saffron risotto. British lamb is best – usually grass-fed and outdoor reared. Great for a winter or early spring supper, I like to garnish it with a zesty mint gremolata for added lift. You might need to ask your butcher ahead of time for this cut. Get them to slice it into roughly 4 cm (2 in) thick slices, or use neck fillet if the bone offends you.

---

1 tablespoon flavourless oil (rapeseed, groundnut or sunflower), plus extra if needed

1 kg (2 lb 3 oz) lamb neck – 4 pieces (about 4 cm/2 in each) with bone in – or neck fillets

sea salt and freshly ground black pepper

1 onion, finely chopped

1 carrot, finely chopped

1 stick celery, finely chopped

3 garlic cloves, peeled and left whole

2 bay leaves

2 sprigs rosemary

2 sprigs thyme, leaves picked

grated zest and juice of 1 unwaxed lemon

8 cherry or small vine tomatoes, halved, or 2 large tomatoes, chopped

1 tablespoon fish sauce

1 tablespoon cider vinegar

150 ml (5 fl oz) dry white wine

MINT GREMOLATA (OPTIONAL GARNISH)

grated zest of ½ unwaxed lemon

1 garlic clove, finely chopped

1 tablespoon finely chopped fresh mint

> Preheat the oven to 160°C (320°F/Gas 2). Heat 1 tablespoon of the oil over a high heat in a large, ovenproof casserole dish. Generously season the lamb pieces all over with salt and pepper, then brown them in batches for a few minutes on each side, to nice, deep brown, transferring them to a plate as you go.

> There should be quite a lot of residual lamb fat in the casserole, but add extra oil if you need to. Turn the heat down to medium and add the onion, carrot and celery. Cook gently for about 10 minutes, stirring occasionally, until they're softened and aromatic, scraping up any brown bits from the lamb that may have stuck to the bottom of the pan (discard anything burned).

> Add the garlic, bay leaves, rosemary and thyme leaves, lemon zest, and tomatoes and cook for a further 5 minutes, stirring, until it's all smelling really good. Pour over the lemon juice, add the fish sauce, wine and vinegar and stir so that all the flavours combine, cooking for a further few minutes. Add the lamb pieces back to the casserole, laying them flat. Pour over the wine and 600 ml (20 fl oz) cold water to cover the meat, and bring the liquid to a boil, then turn down to a simmer. Cover and cook in the oven for 1 hour 30 minutes–2 hours, until the meat is falling off the bone. Cook the risotto [see overleaf] when the lamb has been in the oven for 1 hour.

> To finish the lamb: when you remove it from the oven, remove the lamb pieces from the liquid with a slotted spoon and transfer to a warm plate. Skim off as much surface fat as you can with a large serving spoon, and reduce the braising liquid for about 15 minutes. At this point you can pass the braise through a sieve if you wish to remove the vegetables. Taste for seasoning, and add a dash of vinegar or squeeze of lemon if you think it needs it.

> Mix the gremolata ingredients together in a bowl just before serving and serve the lamb neck on the risotto, with some of the reduced braising liquor poured over, garnished with the mint gremolata (if using).

Pearl barley + squash risotto

20 g (¾ oz) unsalted butter, and 1 extra knob to finish

1 tablespoon olive oil, plus extra if needed

2 small round shallots or 1 banana shallot, finely chopped

2 teaspoons sea salt

2 large sage leaves, finely chopped

1 teaspoon thyme leaves

½ butternut or winter squash peeled, deseeded and cut into 2 cm (1in) cubes

150 g (5 oz/scant ¾ cup) pearl barley

pinch of red chilli flakes

1 litre (34 fl oz) warm chicken stock (preferably home-made, see page 236, but a cube is fine)

40 g (1½ oz) Parmesan, grated

freshly ground black pepper

› Heat the butter and olive oil in a high-sided frying pan (skillet). Add the shallots, 1 teaspoon salt, the sage and thyme and gently sauté for 2 minutes. Increase the heat to medium-high, add the butternut or winter squash and cook for a further 10 minutes.

› Adding a little more oil if necessary, add the pearl barley and chilli flakes, coat in the oil and butter, and cook for 2 minutes. Turn the heat right down and add 1 ladleful of the warm stock, stir and cook until it's absorbed. Continue this process for about 30 minutes or until all of the stock is absorbed and the pearl barley is tender but still a little al dente. Add water if you run out of stock and it still feels like it needs moisture.

› Take the pan off the heat and stir through the Parmesan and butter, and season with salt and pepper.

Chipotle roast chicken

I love the slightly sweet, smoky warmth of the Mexican chipotle chilli: smoke-dried jalapeño. It works really well with the buttery flesh and crispy skin of roast chicken when fashioned into a marinade, and makes for a fun dish for entertaining friends and family. You can get chipotle chillies from specialist Mexican delis or online. I like to serve this 'family style', with the chicken on a big platter in the middle of the table for everyone to help themselves, bowls of warm Cumin and garlic black beans (see page 93), a crunchy salad and corn tortillas.

1 medium (1 kg/2 lb 3 oz), free-range corn-fed chicken

CHIPOTLE MARINADE

2 chipotle chillies, or 2 tablespoons chipotle paste or salsa

juice of ½ lime

1 tablespoon fish sauce

1 tablespoon maple syrup

1 tablespoon rapeseed or olive oil

2 garlic cloves

ICEBERG LETTUCE AND CORIANDER SALAD WITH LIME

1 small iceberg lettuce, washed and shredded

1 red onion, very finely sliced

small bunch of fresh coriander (cilantro) leaves

pinch of caster (superfine) sugar

pinch of sea salt

juice of 1 lime

1 tablespoon extra-virgin olive oil

TO SERVE

corn or wheat tortillas

1 portion of Cumin and garlic black beans (see page 93)

➤ If using chipotle chillies, rehydrate them in a bowl of boiling water for 10–15 minutes, until soft. Blitz all the marinade ingredients together in a food processor and smother the marinade all over the chicken, rubbing it into the skin. Marinate the chicken for 2 hours or overnight in the fridge then bring it up to room temperature by taking it out of the fridge 30 minutes before you cook it.

➤ Preheat the oven to 180°C (350°F/Gas 4).

➤ Put the chicken in a roasting tray and transfer to the oven for 1 hour, removing it to baste it in the juices a couple of times. Remove it from the oven and leave it to rest under some foil. Drain off the juices from the roasting pan, skim off and discard any excess fat and transfer the juices to a bowl or jug, to serve with the chicken.

➤ To make the salad, combine the shredded iceberg, red onion and coriander in a large bowl. To make the dressing, in a bowl, dissolve the salt and sugar in the lime juice and whisk in the olive oil. Dress the salad.

➤ For the tortillas, brush a frying pan (skillet) with the oil and heat until stinking hot. One at a time, toast each tortilla for about 15 seconds (flipping them over to toast both sides), until warm and soft. Serve in a pile.

➤ Carve the chicken and serve on a warmed serving platter, drizzled with its smoky, spicy roasting juices. Serve with bowls of the salad and warmed through Cumin and garlic black beans and tortillas.

Melting Mexican pork tacos with pink pickled onions

A couple of years ago I fulfilled a lifelong dream of going to Mexico. We'd been travelling around the States in cold weather prior to this, and the heat, colour and spirit of the Yucatán Peninsula drew us in. But aside from all the sun, sea and cervesas, it was the food that left the most lasting impression. I'd had good, authentic Mexican food before in London, LA and New York, but this was something else – the vitality and flavour combinations, along with the freshness of the produce and slow cooking methods, blew me away, and I ate tacos practically every day. One of the most ubiquitous dishes of the region is cochinita pibil – a slow-cooked pork dish where pork is marinated in acidic bright red annatto seed paste and slow cooked in banana leaves. The pork is served with tacos, black beans and pink pickled onions and is a total flavour bomb. This is my version, using grapefruit rather than the traditional orange, because my boyfriend is allergic, and it's a great dish to prep ahead and serve when you're entertaining.

MARINADE

40 g (1½ oz) achiote/annatto paste or a blend of 1 teaspoon dried oregano, 1 teaspoon ground cumin, 1 teaspoon black peppercorns and 1 tablespoon hot smoked paprika

½ tablespoon salt

2 garlic cloves

1 bay leaf

1 tablespoon olive oil

1 white onion, roughly chopped

2 tablespoons cider vinegar (do not use if using achiote/annatto paste)

grated zest and juice of 2 pink grapefruits

juice of 1 lime

PORK

1 kg (2 lb 3 oz) boneless pork shoulder or butt, cut into 3 cm (1½ in) chunks

1 white onion, finely sliced

20 g (¾ oz) butter

2 whole fresh red chillies or 1 scotch bonnet, deseeded and finely chopped

PINK PICKLED ONION

1 small red onion, finely sliced

3 black peppercorns

1 clove

1 teaspoon caster (superfine) sugar

½ teaspoon salt

juice of 2 limes

GUACAMOLE

1 tomato, finely chopped

2 ripe avocados, stoned and chopped

1 garlic clove, crushed with ½ teaspoon sea salt

½ red onion, finely chopped

salt and freshly ground black pepper

1 green chilli, deseeded and finely chopped

15 g (½ oz) coriander (cilantro), leaves and stems chopped, and some leaves reserved for garnish

juice of ½ lime

TORTILLAS

1 teaspoon olive oil

6 corn or flour tortillas

TO SERVE

1 iceberg lettuce, washed and finely sliced

1 portion Cumin and garlic black beans (see page 93)

› First, make the marinade. Place the achiote/annatto paste (or spice blend), salt, garlic and bay leaf in a food processor and blitz until the garlic is crushed. Add the oil and onion and blend to a chunky paste, and then the vinegar (if using), zest and citrus juices and blend to make a smooth paste.

› Place the pork in a large bowl, and pour over the marinade. Coat the pork thoroughly, rubbing the marinade in with your hands. Cover and chill for at least 4 hours, preferably overnight. Remove from the oven at least 1 hour before cooking to bring to room temperature. ›››→

> Preheat the oven to 150°C (300°F/Gas 2).

> Put the pork and its marinade in an ovenproof casserole or high-sided baking tray, top with the sliced onion, butter and chillies and cover it tightly with foil. Place the dish in the centre of the oven and cook for about 3 hours, until the pork is so tender that it falls apart when you prod it with a fork.

> While it is cooking make the pink pickled onion. Place the sliced onion in a bowl and cover with boiling water for 1 minute. Drain. Add the spices, sugar, salt and lime juice, and stir to combine. Leave to sit for 1 hour or so, until the onion has turned bright pink. When you're ready to serve, drain on some kitchen paper, to get rid of the brine.

> For the guacamole, put the tomato, avocado, garlic and onion in a bowl and mash together with a fork. Season with sea salt and pepper, then add the chilli, coriander and lime juice and incorporate. Taste for seasoning and garnish with coriander leaves.

> **TIP:** If you're making the guacamole in advance, pop the avocado stone into the bowl with the guacamole and cover with cling film (plastic wrap) to stop it from going brown.

> For the tortillas, brush a frying pan (skillet) with the oil and heat until stinking hot. One at a time, toast each tortilla for about 15 seconds (flipping them over to toast both sides), until warm and soft. Serve in a pile.

> Use 2 forks to pull the pork apart and place it in a bowl in the middle of the table with the warm juices spooned over. Serve with the tortillas and bowls of shredded iceberg lettuce, guacamole, sour cream, Cumin and garlic black beans and pink pickled onions scattered on top.

The pork can be left to SLOW COOK while you get everything else ready.

Vivek Singh's killer vegetable curry (Gajjar mutter tamatar sabzi)

One of the most incredible work trips I ever did was travelling across Rajasthan on the inaugural voyage of the Maharajas Express, billed as India's version of the Orient Express, but not worlds away from Wes Anderson's Darjeeling Ltd. Leading the trip and guiding us through all the amazing food we ate was London chef and restaurateur chef Vivek Singh, who has since become a friend. There is very little this man doesn't know about spices or Indian cuisine, and he has been kind enough to share this recipe for his failsafe vegetable curry, which is cooked in almost every household in northern India (it's generally considered too humble to put on restaurant menus). What I love about this dish is the way it takes prosaic ingredients and elevates them with clever spicing into something very special.

3 tablespoons vegetable or corn oil

1 bay leaf

4 green cardamom pods

1 teaspoon cumin seeds

3 white onions, finely chopped

3 ripe tomatoes, blended to a purée

2.5 cm (1 in) piece of fresh ginger, finely chopped

2 green chillies, cut in half lengthwise

½ teaspoon ground turmeric

½ teaspoon red chilli powder

1 teaspoon ground cumin

1 teaspoon ground coriander

2 teaspoons salt

4 carrots, cut into 1 cm (½ in) dice

200 g (7 oz/1½ cups) garden peas

juice of 1 lemon

2 tablespoons chopped fresh coriander (cilantro) leaves

> Heat the oil in a heavy-based pan, then add the bay leaf, cardamom pods and cumin seeds. Once they start to crackle, add the chopped onions and cook over a medium-high heat until golden brown. Stir in the puréed tomatoes, ginger, green chillies, spices and salt and cook for 8–10 minutes, until the oil begins to separate from the mixture at the edge of the pan. Add the carrots and cook, stirring, for 2 minutes, then add the peas and cook for 3 minutes. Pour in 250 ml (8½ fl oz) water and cook till the vegetables are tender but still retain a little bite. Check the seasoning, then stir in the lemon juice and sprinkle with the chopped coriander. Serve hot with chapattis or naan bread.

> **TIP FROM VIVEK:** If you cut the carrots into smaller 5 mm (¼ in) dice, and cook the mixture without adding any water, then it can be used as a topping for canapés or as a filling for wraps. *Papdi* – wheat crisps, available in Indian supermarkets – topped with this vegetable curry make a good canapé.

CHAPTER 6

Salads + Vegetables

I HAVE MY MUM AND DAD TO THANK FOR MY LOVE OF SALADS AND ALL THINGS VEGETABLE.

My dad had a vegetable patch that provided him with much-needed pastoral catharsis – a break from the grind and stresses of news – and his family with a steady stream of fresh fruit and veg. He grew seasonal crops including peas, runner beans, raspberries, plums and tomatoes, and I loved nothing more than keeping him company as he worked, slyly swiping handfuls of berries or peas and playing with the toads that hopped from beneath flower pots.

My mum has always known how to make the best of our home-grown produce and she was never shy with the butter either (go Mum). So during family dinners, my sister and I would get almost as territorial about the mounds of buttery runner beans and glossy spring greens flecked with black pepper as we would about the pork and crackling or crispy roast potatoes.

That my childhood was never mired by a hatred for boggy, mushy sprouts or cabbage has meant that I've always embraced vegetables in my everyday cooking, something which I'm thankful for because, aside from being healthy and delicious, these are some of the most economical ingredients out there – particularly if you grow them yourself.

Making vegetables a big part of your diet is a great way to cook with the seasons, which bring with them fleeting treats like asparagus, peas or broad (fava) beans that will never taste as good as when they're at their natural peak. With this in mind, feel free to adapt these recipes to work with what's abundant. You'll find combining things that are in season together – like I do in my samphire and Jersey potato recipe – often makes for the best results.

Chefs like Ottolenghi, Jamie Oliver and Hugh Fearnley-Whittingstall have changed the way we view the humble veg by showing us that you can be just as creative and daring with it as any other ingredient – you just need to be clever about the way you treat it. When paired with things like pulses, nuts, seeds, spices and good cheeses, and sometimes just good butter, vegetables can be elevated from an accompaniment to the main event.

But this chapter isn't just about the veg. You'll find a luxurious seafood salad made with orzo – that smooth, rice-shaped pasta – and there's also an octopus salad which I'd really encourage you to try your hand at. Once you've had a go at prepping this amazing, eight-armed creature, and mastered the method for cooking it to supple tenderness, you'll be equipped with the skills to start making your own octopus dishes, and if you're anything like me, you'll never look back.

Fig, rocket + Gorgonzola salad with toasted almonds + maple dressing

Lots of the stores in my area of north-east London are Turkish-run, so I never have to go very far for one of my all-time favourites: soft, sweet, fresh figs. One of the simplest, tastiest ways to use them is as the basis for a salad. Because they're naturally sweet, figs work best mixed with other bold ingredients like peppery rocket (arugula), salty blue cheese such as Gorgonzola, and a simple dressing of lemon juice and olive oil, sweetened with maple syrup.

DRESSING

1 tablespoon freshly
squeezed lemon juice

1 tablespoon maple syrup

2 tablespoons olive oil

pinch of salt

SALAD

30 g (1 oz/⅓ cup) flaked
almonds

6 ripe figs

100 g (3½ oz) rocket
(arugula)

sea salt and freshly ground
black pepper

40 g (1½ oz) Gorgonzola
cheese, torn into pieces

> Whisk all the dressing ingredients together in a small bowl and set aside.

> Put the flaked almonds in a dry non-stick frying pan (skillet) and toast over a medium heat for a few minutes, until they're golden but not too dark brown. Transfer to a bowl and set aside.

> Slice the figs. Lay them and the rocket on a salad plate, toss with the lemon and maple dressing, and season with a little salt and pepper. Scatter over the Gorgonzola and toasted almonds and serve.

Octopus, avocado + butter bean salad with a chilli garlic dressing

When cooked slowly and carefully, octopus achieves a tender yet substantial quality unlike any other seafood, and once you've braised it in its own juices using the method below, you can finish it on a barbecue for a smoky char, fry it in a bit of olive oil to crisp it up at the edges, or keep it in the fridge and use it as a protein ingredient as and when. My method is adapted from Anna Hansen's recipe in her book The Modern Pantry, which is in turn adapted from Giorgio Locatelli's method in Made In Italy: Food and Other Stories. I use the softened garlic and chillies cooked with the octopus, and the wonderfully flavourful juices released during cooking to make a punchy dressing for this salad of beans and avocado. It's worth eating it with bread to mop up the dressing.

OCTOPUS

1 octopus (about 1 kg/2 lb 3 oz)

8 tablespoons olive oil

2 red bird's-eye chillies, halved

5 garlic cloves, peeled and left whole

3 slices of lemon

few sprigs flat-leaf parsley, leaves and stems

1 bay leaf

3 black peppercorns

SALAD

handful of cherry tomatoes, halved

extra-virgin olive oil

sea salt

1 sprig rosemary, leaves picked and chopped

2 teaspoons white wine vinegar

juice of ½ lemon

pinch of ground white pepper

400 g (14 oz) tin butter beans, drained and rinsed

½ red onion, finely chopped

handful of flat-leaf parsley leaves, roughly chopped

1 ripe avocado, peeled, stoned and cubed

> First you need to tenderise the octopus. You can do this very easily by freezing it a couple of days before you cook it, and then defrosting it. I tend to buy it frozen from the fishmonger (lots of Asian grocers also sell them frozen) so I just need to defrost it and I'm ready to go. You may also need to remove the eyes. Do this by cutting around and under them with a very sharp knife and popping them and the attached cartilage out. When you cut out the eyes you can then press the hard beak (the creature's mouth) out of the centre cavity where the legs join together. Clean any gunk from the cavities with kitchen paper, and rinse the octopus under cold water in the sink for about 10 minutes. Alternatively, ask your fishmonger to clean and prep the octopus for you.

> Place 6 tablespoons of the olive oil with the octopus, chillies, garlic, lemon slices, parsley, bay leaf and peppercorns in a large pot or casserole, give it a shake, and cover tightly with a lid. Slowly bring it up to the boil and simmer gently for 30 minutes. At this point check for tenderness, prodding a skewer or cocktail stick into the fattest part of the octopus. If the octopus falls off the skewer easily with little resistance, rather than sticking to it, it's done. If it clings to the skewer, cook it for a further 10–15 minutes, or until there's no resistance.

> While the octopus is cooking, toss the tomatoes in 1 tablespoon of extra-virgin olive oil with a pinch of sea salt, the rosemary and vinegar and set aside. >>>➤

> Once it's cooked until tender, transfer the octopus from the casserole to a plate. Allow it to cool and then, if you like, peel off the dark skin and cut into chunks – I like to keep some of the arms intact for presentation. To make the chilli garlic dressing, place the softened garlic and cooked chillies that were cooked with the octopus in mini-chopper with about 5 tablespoons of the purple cooking liquor from the pot and blitz until you have a creamy, emulsified sauce. Add the remaining 2 tablespoons of olive oil, the lemon juice and white pepper, and blitz again. Taste for seasoning – you might need to add more lemon juice if it tastes too salty, or more olive oil if it's a little sharp. Use your judgment to adjust the dressing.

> To assemble the salad, mix the beans with the onion, parsley, avocado and marinated tomatoes, and arrange on the plate. Top with the octopus, and drizzle with the dressing.

> **TIP:** If you have any leftover octopus, try brushing it with olive oil and grilling it on a barbecue, then serving it dressed with lemon, olive oil, paprika and parsley or salsa verde. Or, fry it up with some potatoes and chorizo, like they do in Spain, and garnish with the chilli garlic dressing.

Warm salad of roasted aubergine + broccoli with anchovy lemon dressing

This is one of the most popular recipes from the blog and I think that's because it's super wholesome and nutritious but tasty and sating at the same time. It centers around the badass brassica broccoli: one of the foods I really crave when I've been overindulging, which, as you know, happens fairly regularly. I love the nutty flavour broccoli takes on when you roast it in a bit of olive oil in a hot oven: it's more interesting and satisfying than just blanching it, and it retains its crunch a little better, which works really well against the squish of the roasted aubergine (eggplant). This recipe uses the stalks and leaves of the broccoli too as they're just as yummy as the florets and too good to waste.

SALAD

1 medium aubergine
 (eggplant)

extra virgin olive oil

½ teaspoon of sea salt

1 teaspoon dried
red chilli flakes

half a head of broccoli

2 handfuls of baby
spinach leaves

DRESSING

juice of ½ lemon

2 tablespoons extra
virgin olive oil

splash of tabasco

½ teaspoon honey

1 teaspoon tahini

½ a small tin of anchovies
in olive oil, chopped
handful of flat leaf parsley,
finely chopped

sea salt and black pepper

> Preheat the oven to 180ºC (350ºF/Gas 4).

> Slice the aubergine into hearty rounds (about 2–3 cm/1–1.5 in thick). In a bowl, coat the aubergine in the oil, salt and chilli. Then lay them onto a flat baking tray and place in the hot oven for 10 minutes.

> In the meantime, cut the florets of broccoli off the stalk, reserving the stalk and any leaves, as these can be roasted too. Cut the broccoli florets into bite-sized pieces. People tend to throw the stalk away, but it's actually just as tasty as the rest of this brassica if you get to the tender inside bit, so waste not, want not. Cut off the rough end of the stalk, and peel with a knife until you get to the tender pale bit inside. Slice into 2 cm (1 in) thick rectangles.

> After the aubergine has cooked for 10 minutes, remove the tray from the oven and turn the rounds over. Place the broccoli stalks, florets and leaves in a roasting tray, toss with salt, pepper and olive oil and place in the oven with the aubergine for 15–20 minutes, until the aubergine is soft and golden brown and the broccoli is tinged brown. You may need to remove the leaves early, to avoid them burning.

> To make the dressing combine the lemon juice, olive oil, tabasco, honey and tahini in a bowl, until it's all emulsified and then add in the chopped anchovies, and parsley.

> When the vegetables are ready, take them out of the oven and let them sit for 5 minutes. Arrange the baby spinach on the plate, scatter over the aubergine and broccoli, and drizzle over your dressing. This dish works well on its own as a healthy supper, or on the side with something like roast lamb.

Shredded sprout salad, two ways

*S*prouts are delicious thinly sliced and eaten raw. Crunchy, nutty and satisfying, they're a great vehicle for interesting dressings and creamy blue cheese. I discovered sprout salads when living in North America, where sprouts don't have the soggy school dinner associations they have in the UK, and are as cool as kale. I say embrace these miraculous little cabbages! They're cheap, healthy, keep well and are really versatile – what's not to like? Sprout salads are a brilliant way to use up any that you might have lying around in your fridge. Just the thing for a nourishing little lunch. I've given you two options for dressings here – a simple, fresh citrus one (pictured), and a spicy buttermilk version – so you can vary how you dress the salad according to how you feel.

100 g (3½ oz) Brussels sprouts, washed, peeled and finely sliced from the top of the sprout to the base

1 shallot, very finely sliced

1 tablespoon finely chopped fresh flat-leaf parsley leaves

1 tablespoon finely chopped fresh mint

generous pinch of red chilli flakes (leave out if using spicy buttermilk dressing)

sea salt and freshly ground black pepper

15 g (½ oz) acidic, crumbly blue cheese (I like Wensleydale blue or Stilton), if using

40 g (1½ oz/scant ½ cup) toasted flaked almonds or toasted pumpkin seeds

CITRUS DRESSING

pinch of salt

juice of ½ lemon

1 teaspoon honey or maple syrup

2 teaspoons Dijon mustard

2 tablespoons olive oil

BUTTERMILK AND JALAPEÑO DRESSING

2 jalapeño chillies, deseeded and chopped

2 teaspoons fresh lime juice

4 tablespoons finely chopped fresh coriander (cilantro) leaves

50 ml (2 fl oz) sour cream

50 ml (2 fl oz) buttermilk

½ teaspoon garlic granules

½ teaspoon ground cumin

¼ teaspoon dried oregano

½ teaspoon salt, or to taste

➤ Combine the sliced sprouts, shallot and herbs in a large bowl. Season with chilli flakes (if using), salt and pepper.

➤ To make the citrus dressing, dissolve the salt in the lemon juice and taste – you don't want it to be bracingly acidic. Add more salt to balance if needed. Whisk in the honey or maple syrup, Dijon mustard and finally the olive oil. Taste the dressing and adjust the seasoning accordingly.

➤ To make the spicy jalapeño buttermilk dressing, combine all the dressing ingredients in the bowl of a food processor, and blitz until smooth.

➤ Dress the sprout salad and lightly pile it onto plates. Crumble over the blue cheese, if you have used the citrus dressing. Leave out the blue cheese if you have used the jalapeño dressing.

➤ Garnish with the toasted almonds or pumpkin seeds and enjoy!

I've *always* liked my food!

Mum's seafood orzo salad

My mum got the idea of an orzo-based seafood salad from her seafood hero, the legend that is Rick Stein. But having made variations of it over the years based on what she gets fresh from her fishmonger in the seaside town of Deal in Kent, I think she can claim this particular version as her own by now. This is her standard dish for entertaining friends, and it always goes down a storm, thanks to the way she lightly cooks the seafood so that even when it's prepped ahead and served at room temperature it's absolutely delicious. You can adapt it according to what you can source and what you fancy – I sometimes add clams, cockles or little brown shrimp, and it's also perfectly lovely with mussels.

200 g (7 oz) cherry
tomatoes, halved

extra-virgin olive oil

sea salt and freshly
ground black pepper

1 teaspoon fresh thyme leaves

300 g (10½ oz) cleaned squid
(ask your fishmonger to
clean it for you)

grated zest and juice of
1 unwaxed lemon

2 garlic cloves, crushed

10 g (½ oz) pine nuts

5 spring onions (scallions),
finely sliced

300 g (10½ oz) orzo pasta

1 red chilli, deseeded
and finely sliced

1 green chilli, deseeded
and finely sliced

12 raw king prawns, shells on

300 g (10½ oz) shelled,
cooked prawns

1 tablespoon finely chopped
flat-leaf parsley leaves

1 tablespoon finely chopped
chives

> Preheat the oven to 140°C (280°F/Gas 1).

> Coat the tomato halves in 1 tablespoon of olive oil, lay on a baking sheet, season with salt and pepper, and scatter over the thyme leaves. Roast for 1 hour, until slightly shrivelled, concentrated and softened. Remove from the oven and set aside.

> Now prepare the squid. Keep the tentacles whole, because they look good in a salad, but with a sharp knife, cut the body pouches down one side, wiping with kitchen paper, and open them out on a chopping board. Remove any leftover membrane or innards, and lightly score with a cross-hatch pattern with the tip of the knife. Cut the squid into 5 cm (2 in) pieces and put them in a bowl with 1 tablespoon of olive oil, a squeeze of lemon juice, salt and pepper, and 1 teaspoon of the crushed garlic.

> Cover and leave to marinate while you prep the other ingredients.

> Put the pine nuts in a dry frying pan (skillet) over a medium heat, and toast them until golden, tossing them in the pan occasionally. Remove and set aside.

> Heat 1 tablespoon of olive oil in the frying pan over a low heat, add the spring onions and cook for about 4 minutes, until they're soft but not golden. Set aside.

> Cook the orzo pasta in a very large saucepan of boiling water, according to packet instructions (normally 5–6 minutes), until al dente. Drain and rinse under cold water. Transfer to a large bowl, and, once cool, pour over a glug of olive oil and fork through the pasta to separate the 'grains'. »»→

> Heat some more olive oil in a wok or heavy-based frying pan (skillet) until very hot. Add half the chopped red and green chillies, followed by the squid, and cook, shaking the pan or using a wooden spoon to stir fry it for about 2 minutes. The body sections should curl up into tubes. Remove from the pan with a slotted spoon and set aside.

> Adding a little bit more oil if you need to, cook the king prawns in the wok or frying pan (skillet) for about 4 minutes until they turn red. When they are cool enough to handle, peel most of them

and remove the black intestinal tract running down the back of them with a sharp knife. You can leave a couple in the shell for presentation.

> Once cooled slightly, mix the squid, king prawns and shelled prawns, remaining chilli, lemon zest and remaining juice, parsley, tomatoes, pine nuts and spring onions into the orzo. Garnish with chives, season with salt and pepper, and drizzle over a touch more olive oil.

I like HEIRLOOM tomatoes because of their interesting shapes + colours.

Panzanella

When I discovered this traditional Tuscan tomato and bread salad it was love at first taste. It's an ingenious way to use up those stale bits of sourdough or crusty bread you might have lurking in your kitchen, which, when soaked in the sweet tomato juices, become absolutely delicious. Because this dish is so simple, it's important to use the best ripe tomatoes, olive oil and bread you can find. I like heirloom tomato varieties, if I can track them down, because of their interesting shapes and colours, and they tend to have a more pronounced flavour. Sourdough works wonderfully too. This dish is best in the summer, when tomatoes are at their best.

handful of fresh basil (about 12 g/½ oz)

4 tablespoons extra-virgin olive oil, plus extra for drizzling

1 tablespoon salted capers, rinsed

300 g (10½ oz) stale sourdough, torn into chunks

500 g (1 lb 2 oz) ripe heirloom tomatoes (a variety of colours, shapes and sizes), washed and sliced, reserving the seeds and juice

10 g (½ oz) kalamata or other dark olives, pitted and sliced

½ red onion, finely sliced

sea salt and freshly ground black pepper

1 tablespoon red wine vinegar

> Blitz most of the basil leaves (leave a few whole for garnish) in a food processor with the olive oil and capers, or finely chop the basil and capers together by hand and stir into the olive oil if you prefer. Transfer to a bowl and add the sourdough chunks. Toss them in the herby caper oil.

> Place the tomatoes, squeezing some of them to release their juice, in a large salad bowl along with the reserved seeds and juice, and mix with most of the olives and red onion, and some more olive oil. Season with salt and pepper and add the vinegar, stirring to coat. Add half of the herby caper oil and all of the sourdough, and mix to make sure the bread is coated in all the juices.

> To serve, transfer the salad to a serving platter, layering the tomato slices, olives, onion and sourdough. Drizzle over the remaining herb oil and garnish with fresh basil leaves and the remaining red onion and olives. Season again with salt and pepper and devour immediately.

Asparagus with charred lemon butter + Parmesan

A *s soon as the short asparagus season starts, I find myself eating the tender green spears at every given opportunity. To make the most of their incredibly special flavour, I like to keep things simple, and this is one of my favourite preparations – good for a quick lunch or an easy starter. Charring the lemon caramelises it, adding bitter notes and heightening its sweetness, giving it a complexity that works well with the salty Parmesan and nutty asparagus.*

400 g (14 oz) asparagus spears

1 lemon, halved

olive oil

15 g (½ oz) unsalted butter

salt and freshly ground black pepper

40 g (1½ oz) Parmesan

› Snap the woody bases from the asparagus spears, keeping only the tender tips. Heat a non-stick frying pan (skillet) or griddle pan until stinking hot. Brush the lemon halves with a little bit of olive oil and place cut-side down on the pan. Cook for about 5 minutes, until the cut sides of the lemons are caramelised and charred, then set aside.

› Melt the butter in the lemon pan. When cool enough to handle, squeeze in the charred lemon juice and stir to incorporate over the heat.

› Bring a large pan of salted water to the boil and add the asparagus tips, cooking for 2 minutes, or until tender. Drain in a colander and toss them immediately into the lemon butter, over a very low heat. Divide between plates, season with black pepper and grate over the Parmesan. Eat immediately, with your fingers.

Summer watermelon, feta + radish salad with mint

I really got into eating watermelon during the sweltering summer I spent in Vancouver, when sinking my teeth into the sweet, juicy flesh became a refreshing way to cool down. This summery salad is great as a starter or light lunch, and works well with barbecued meats, too.

500 g (1 lb 2 oz) watermelon flesh, pips removed and cut into cubes or chunks

150 g (5 oz) feta, *queso blanco* (Mexican soft cheese) or other salty fresh white cheese, diced

½ red onion, finely sliced

juice of ½ lime

freshly ground white pepper

olive oil

3 red radishes, very finely sliced

bunch of mint, leaves picked over and stems removed

❯ Combine the watermelon, cheese and red onion in a bowl, and toss with the lime juice, white pepper and olive oil. Transfer to a plate, scatter over the radish slices and mint leaves, and serve.

Jersey Royals with samphire

As soon as Jersey Royal potatoes are in season, I get myself to the greengrocer and buy them by the bag. There's just no other potato like them (although Yukon Gold is the closest contender): they are the simplest of nature's pleasures, and I like to celebrate them in their own right, allowing their intensely earthy, potato flavour to sing. Because Jerseys are traditionally grown with seaweed in the soil, I find it fitting to cook them with a bit of juicy samphire. This makes a really good accompaniment to a simple grilled fish supper, but is also a nice little lunch all by itself.

350 g (12 oz) Jersey Royals (or Yukon Gold, or other new season potatoes), washed and scrubbed lightly to remove any soil

100 g (3½ oz) samphire

knob of unsalted butter

sea salt and freshly ground black pepper

squeeze of lemon juice

➤ Put the potatoes in a large saucepan, fill it with cold water and add 2 large pinches of salt. Bring it up to the boil, skimming the surface of any impurities, and cook for 15–20 minutes, until the potatoes are squashable with your fingers. Don't be afraid of overcooking them; you want them tender, not in any way al dente. Just before you drain them, add the samphire into the cooking stock and blanch for about 1 minute, then drain. Transfer to a large bowl, add the butter, tossing to coat, and season with salt and pepper. Squeeze over some lemon juice, and serve while hot.

CHAPTER 7

Desserts
+drinks

I'VE ALWAYS BEEN A SUCKER FOR A PUD, AND AS MUCH AS I LOVE A CHEESEBOARD, I'M NOT ONE OF THOSE 'I'LL SKIP DESSERT' TYPES.

I'll take dessert and then some cheese please. Simple, seasonal sweets float my boat, probably because that's the way I grew up eating: raiding the cherry, pear and plum trees in our garden as soon as their spoils were ripe for the picking.

Now I live in the city, it's the greengrocers and markets I raid (don't worry, I always pay), but I still like to work with whatever fruit is abundant at the time: you get fruit at its prime and it ends up costing less. That said, I'm not puritanical about it, so you'll notice that a couple of these puddings rely on tinned fruit, which I find can be really handy to have in the cupboard for when you get a craving for something sweet, or during the colder months when exciting fruit is a bit thin on the ground. The Elderflower cordial on page 226 also features, because its sweet, summery, floral notes are perfect for desserts.

When it comes to baking, I've taken my lead from the pies and puddings I ate while living in Canada, where I found myself surrounded by artisan bakeries and coffee shops selling the most wonderful array of bakes and sweet treats. My cherry pie is a version of a dish I ate loads of while living there, because fruit pies are a north American staple, and it was inspiring to see how the locals adapted them with the

seasons, filling them with the fuzzy white peaches, deep purple cherries and the plumpest, juiciest blueberries. In Vancouer there was even a *Twin Peaks*-themed bar that sold cherry pie by the slice, along with cups of 'joe' (coffee).

I spent some time helping (or quite possibly hindering) the pastry chefs at a local patisserie called Thierry, where I was shown how to properly handle a piping bag and tasked with making macarons. One of my favourites was filled with a gorgeous lemon curd and maraschino cherries, and I've taken those flavours and used them for the basis of my super-simple Lemon meringue posset on page 220.

My mum has also had a big impact on what I cherish for pudding, and she instilled in me a healthy love of fluffy, perfectly whipped cream and light, squidgy meringues, which both come into play in this chapter. She also introduced me, and many of my friends, to the delights of lychees, which were still quite exotic and unusual when I was growing up. They're the centrepiece of the Hazelnut pavlova on page 209, and as much as I love them, they'll always remind me of the Halloween parties we used to have where my mum would fill bowls with them and ask my friends to try them blindfold, telling them they were eyeballs. It never seemed to put anyone off her pavlova though.

Salted butterscotch popcorn cheesecake

I t's no secret among those who know me that I love popcorn. I even made-up a song about it once. During university, I spent a little too much time going to the cinema, which gave me an excuse to eat unreasonable quantities of popcorn. I just find it utterly addictive. Luckily, thanks to it becoming rather a trendy restaurant 'snack' in recent years, rather than finding its presence in my life has dwindled, I've actually never eaten more of the stuff. This dessert pays homage to it, the popcorn providing a crunchy vehicle for an evil salted butterscotch sauce. It's basically toffee popcorn in an easy, no-bake cheesecake, and, once made, it doesn't last more than a day in my fridge. It's also best eaten the day you make it, as the popcorn loses its crunch when kept in the fridge for days. If you want to make it ahead, omit the popcorn from the base, reserve half of the butterscotch sauce for the topping, and put freshly popped popcorn on the top of the cake on the day, then smother it in the sauce.

POPCORN

1 tablespoon flavourless oil
(groundnut or sunflower)

large pinch of sea salt

40 g (1½ oz/¼ cup) popcorn
maize kernels

CHEESECAKE

200 g (7 oz) digestive biscuits

small handful of popcorn (see above)

pinch of sea salt

100 g (3½ oz) butter, melted,
plus extra for greasing

500 g (1 lb 2 oz/2 cups)
mascarpone or soft cheese

100 g (3½ oz/generous ⅓ cup)
quark

80 g (3 oz) icing (confectioners') sugar,
plus extra to taste

100 ml (3½ fl oz) double (heavy) cream

SALTED BUTTERSCOTCH SAUCE

30 g (1 oz) unsalted butter, diced

1 teaspoon milk

160 ml (5¼ fl oz) double (heavy) cream

145 g (5 oz/¾ cup) light muscovado sugar

generous pinch of sea salt

SPECIAL EQUIPMENT

20 cm (8 in) springform cake tin

› First, make the popcorn. Put a large pot with a lid over a medium-high heat and add the oil and salt. Drop in a couple of popcorn kernels and cover the pan with a lid. When the kernels start to pop, add the rest of the corn and cover with the lid. Shake the pan to evenly coat the kernels, and leave to heat up, shaking the pan around gently when it starts popping, to make sure the un-popped kernels get to the heat, and the popped ones don't burn on the bottom of the pan. Set the lid slightly ajar to release some of the steam and make crisper popcorn. Once the popcorn has stopped popping every few seconds, take it off the heat and leave it to one side until all the popping has stopped completely.

› Grease the cake tin and line the base and sides with greaseproof paper.

› To make the cheesecake base, put the biscuits in a sealed food bag and smash them with a rolling pin into crumbs, or put them in a food processor and grind to coarse crumbs. Transfer to a mixing bowl and stir in a small handful of popcorn and a pinch of sea salt.

› Melt the butter in a saucepan over a low heat and pour it over the crumbs. Mix it all together with a fork and put your mixture into the cake tin. Tap the side of the tin with the flat of your hand to even it out and ⟫⟶

gently compress the mixture with the back of a large spoon until it's packed in and level. You want it fairly well packed so that it holds together. Transfer to the fridge to cool.

> To make the salted butterscotch sauce, melt the butter, milk, cream, sugar and salt together in a medium non-stick saucepan, and, stirring continuously, bring to the boil. Although it may look super tempting, don't swipe your finger over the spoon: flesh and boiling sugar don't mix. Turn down to a simmer and cook for 10 minutes, stirring occasionally. Remove from the heat and set to one side. If, when it's cooler, the mixture is stiff, warm it up over the heat with a splash of milk to loosen it. You want it still warm and runny so that you can pour it over the cheesecake.

> Put the mascarpone or soft cheese, quark and icing sugar into a mixing bowl or the bowl of a stand mixer, and beat it together. If you don't have a stand mixer use an electric hand whisk. Mix until it's well combined and thickening, then add the cream and continue to mix. You want it thick, but not over-whipped. Pour in about half the salted butterscotch sauce, and fold it through the cream cheese mixture to create a ripple effect. Taste it and add more butterscotch sauce or salt if you feel it needs it.

> Pile the mixture on top of the buttery biscuit base and smooth it down with the back of the spoon or a palette knife. Cover with cling film (plastic wrap) and chill for at least 2 hours, then scatter the rest of the popcorn over the top, drizzle with the remaining butterscotch sauce, and serve.

Cherry pie

No one does fruit pies quite like our cousins across the pond. When we were living in North America, I ate more than my fair share of pie. I couldn't pass a bakery or coffee shop without being lured in by golden sugared crusts spilling with deep, bubbling, sweet fruit fillings. In Vancouver there was a wonderful little place called the Olde Pie Shoppe, which just served freshly baked, seasonal fruit pies and very good pour-over coffee – a genius idea. This is my version of the ubiquitous cherry pie. I use a small heart-shaped cookie cutter to make holes in the top crust, and it always goes down a storm. Eat it with a mug of 'joe', like they do in Twin Peaks.

PASTRY

2 tablespoons granulated sugar

260 g (9 oz/2 cups) plain (all-purpose) flour, plus extra for dusting

40 g (1½ oz/generous ⅓ cup) ground almonds

pinch of salt

180 g (6 oz) cold unsalted butter, cut into cubes

1 large egg, beaten

1 tablespoon demerara (raw) sugar, for sprinkling

FILLING

100 g (3½ oz) good-quality black cherry jam

1 tablespoon cherry brandy, kirsch or amaretto (optional)

½ teaspoon grated nutmeg

½ teaspoon vanilla extract

1 tablespoon cornflour (cornstarch), mixed to a paste with 2 teaspoons cold water

500 g (1 lb 2 oz) fresh black or red cherries, pitted and halved

SPECIAL EQUIPMENT

24 cm (10 in) pie dish

pastry brush

> For the pastry, put the sugar, flour, ground almonds, salt and butter in a food processor, and blitz until the mixture resembles fine breadcrumbs. With the motor still running, add about 3 tablespoons of the beaten egg and 2 tablespoons of ice-cold water, and pulse until the mixture starts to clump together into a dough. You need to be cautious at this stage as you don't want sticky pastry. Add a little more water if necessary.

> Remove the dough from the food processor, divide into two, flatten each portion into discs, wrap each disc in cling film and chill in the fridge for at least 1 hour.

> Preheat the oven to 200°C (400°F/Gas 6) and grease the pie dish. Remove a disc of pastry from the fridge, unwrap it and roll it out on a generously floured work surface to 3 mm (⅛ in) thick and about 2½ cm (1 in) wider than the pie dish. Transfer to a floured baking sheet and chill for about 10 minutes. Repeat this process with the remaining disc of pastry.

> Heat the jam for the filling in a saucepan with 100 ml (3½ fl oz) water, the alcohol (if using), nutmeg and the vanilla extract. When it's all melted together, add the diluted cornflour, and stir together until smooth and thickened. Add the cherries and gently coat them in the mixture, being careful not to mush them up, so you preserve their shape. Remove from the heat and set aside.

> Using a floured rolling pin, carefully transfer one of the chilled pastry sheets to the greased pie dish and drape it across the dish. Let it sink into the dish, and, holding on to the edges, lift and tuck the pastry into the edges of the dish, all the way round, to line it. Trim off any excess pastry, and lightly prick the base with a fork. Fill the dish with the cherry filling. Use a pastry cutter to cut holes in the remaining pastry sheet, covering an area just smaller than the diameter of the pie dish, leaving a large border intact. Place it over the pie filling, and fold the edge of the top crust over the edge of the bottom crust, crimping it together with your fingers to seal.

> Brush the pastry with the remains of the beaten egg and sprinkle over the demerara sugar. Bake for 20 minutes, until the crust is golden, and then reduce the oven temperature to 180°C (350°F/Gas 4), covering the top of the pastry with foil if you need to, to avoid it burning, and bake for a further 35–40 minutes, until the filling is bubbling and the pastry is golden, firm and lightly puffed. Allow the pie to cool for about 1 hour before serving with cream.

lychee + hazelnut pavlova

I can't take credit for this creation – this is one of my mum's inventions and it was a real favourite of ours growing up, thanks to its gorgeous combination of soft, crunchy, hazelnut-flecked meringue, clouds of whipped cream and sweet, floral lychees. Because it's a quick-cook pavlova it will come out of the oven crackled and beautifully soft in the middle, so be very careful how you handle it. Hilariously, I once tried to recreate it in a home economics class at school, where we'd been asked to bake a recipe of our choice. My teacher, a terrifyingly shrill, screeching woman with, as far as I could tell, no natural instinct for food or flavour, read the recipe and insisted that I wouldn't be able to bake a pavlova in 35 minutes. Outraged, she threw my mix away and sent me home in tears. This one's for you, Miss Clarkson.

MERINGUE

4 medium egg whites,
at room temperature

250 g (9 oz/generous cup)
caster (superfine) sugar

3–4 drops vanilla extract

½ teaspoon white
wine vinegar

125 g (4 oz) toasted
hazelnuts, roughly
chopped

FILLING + TOPPING

300 ml (10 fl oz) double
(heavy) cream

425 g (15 oz) tin lychees
in syrup

icing (confectioners')
sugar, for dusting

flesh and seeds of
3 passionfruits

> Preheat the oven to 170°C (335°F/Gas 3½) and line two baking sheets with baking parchment.

> Whisk the egg whites in a spotlessly clean bowl with an electric mixer or in a stand mixer until thick and fluffy and soft peaks form, then gradually add the sugar, a little at a time, whisking constantly until thick and glossy. Whisk in the vanilla extract and vinegar and gently fold in the chopped nuts.

> Spread a circle of meringue, 20–25 cm (8–10 in) in diameter, on each baking sheet. Bake for 35–40 minutes (don't worry if the top cracks, it will still taste delightful), until they easily peel away from the parchment. Remove from the oven and carefully lift the meringues and baking parchment onto a wire rack and rest until they've cooled. Peel the parchment from the meringue discs and – using a palette knife – lift one onto a serving platter or cake stand.

> Whip the cream into soft peaks, being careful not to over-whip, and drain the lychees, reserving the juice. Gently fold three quarters of the lychees into the cream with 1–2 teaspoons of the lychee juice (the mixture will thicken). Spread most of the cream and lychee mixture onto the base meringue, saving some to cover the top layer, and sandwich with the other meringue. Pile the remaining cream mix onto the top meringue and cover with the remaining lychees and passionfruit flesh and seeds, and dust with icing sugar.

Black cherry brûlée

This was one of my favourite desserts growing up, and crushing through the glass-like sugar top down into the mounds of cream was always something I savoured when my mum made it. It's so simple, but there's something about the shards of crunchy brûlée, the soft, sumptuous black cherries and their deep purple juices all melded with clouds of cream, slightly sharpened by yoghurt, that's just an absolute winner. This is a good dessert to make ahead.

200 ml (7 fl oz) double (heavy) cream

300 g (10½ oz/1¼ cups) thick Greek yoghurt (full fat, don't scrimp on this one)

215 g (7½ oz) drained, tinned, pitted black cherries, with 2 tablespoons juice/syrup reserved, or a 200 g (7 oz) mix of fresh raspberries and fresh pitted cherries

1 tablespoon cassis, cherry brandy or kirsch

70 g (2½ oz/⅓ cup) demerara (raw) sugar

➤ Whip the cream until just past the soft peak stage, so it's thick but not quite stiff. Fold it into the yoghurt until it's smooth and well incorporated. Put the cherries (or fresh raspberries and cherries), the reserved juice and the alcohol into the bottom of an oven/grill-proof serving dish and stir to coat. Top with the yoghurt and cream mixture and scatter over the sugar in an even layer. Place under a hot grill (or use a blow torch) to toast the sugar until it's bubbling and brûléed – its individual grains should have melded into a hot molten layer. DO NOT test it with your finger. Leave for at least 20 minutes, until it's completely set and cooled, and chill until you are ready to serve.

Orange + ginger madeleines

These fluffy, buttery little French sponges will always remind me of long car journeys across France during our family camping holidays. We'd buy them by the bagful from French hypermarkets, and my sister and I would chomp our way through them while listening to our Walkman cassette players and poring over puzzle books. In my adult life, I've eaten rather more refined versions at wonderful restaurants like St. John in Clerkenwell or my pal James Lowe's restaurant Lyle's in Shoreditch. My favourites though, were those I ate straight from the oven at Thierry patisserie in Vancouver, where I helped out for a few days. This warming version is flavoured with orange and stem ginger.

100 g (3½ oz) unsalted butter, melted and cooled, plus extra for greasing

plain (all-purpose) flour, for dusting

2 medium eggs

100 g (3½ oz/scant ½ cup) caster (superfine) sugar

80 g (3 oz/⅔ cup) self-raising flour, sifted

20 g (¾ oz/¼ cup) ground almonds

2 teaspoons ground ginger

pinch of salt

2 balls preserved stem ginger in syrup, finely chopped

grated zest of 1 orange

1 tablespoon orange juice

SPECIAL EQUIPMENT

12-hole madeleine tin

› Grease the madeleine tin with butter then sprinkle with a light dusting of plain flour.

› Place the eggs and sugar in a mixing bowl and whisk by hand or in the bowl of a stand mixer until pale and fluffy, and then fold in the remaining ingredients until you have a smooth batter. Leave the batter to sit for 30 minutes, and preheat the oven to 200°C (400°F/Gas 6).

› Spoon (or, if you have a piping bag, pipe) just under 1 tablespoon of the mixture into each hole in the madeleine tin – being sure not to overfill each hole (you need less mixture than you might think because it will puff up). Bake in the oven for 8–10 minutes, until golden brown.

› Once baked, remove the madeleines from the tin and leave to cool on a wire rack. Or just scoff them while they're warm. I would.

Blueberry, basil + almond pudding pie

I'd never tasted blueberries like the ones I ate in Vancouver, where punnets of them set you back just a few bucks during the summer season. Baked into this simple dessert with ground almonds and fragrant basil leaves, they make for a squishy, sweet, gorgeously light dessert that's just the ticket for summer. I use half ground almonds and half whole, skin-on blitzed-up almonds to give a bit of texture and rusticity, and the result is rather lovely – the squidgy, ever-so-sweet fruit melding with the sponge and the crunchy almonds.

softened butter, for greasing

5 large basil leaves

380 g (13 oz) blueberries

20 g (¾ oz/scant ¼ cup)
plain (all-purpose) flour, sifted

½ teaspoon baking powder

90 g (3¼ oz/scant cup)
ground almonds

90 g (3¼ oz/½ cup) whole,
skin-on almonds, blitzed
until roughly ground

60 g (2 oz/¼ cup) golden
caster (superfine) sugar

4 eggs, at room temperature

sour cream, plain yoghurt or crème
fraîche, to serve

SPECIAL
EQUIPMENT

20 cm (8 in) round springform
cake tin or flan dish

> Preheat the oven to 180°C (350°F). Grease the cake tin or flan dish with butter and place the basil leaves on the bottom of it. Pour over the blueberries and set aside. Combine the flour, baking powder and almonds. In another bowl whisk the sugar and eggs for about 3 minutes until frothy. Gently fold in the flour and almonds, keeping as much air in the mixture as you can. Pour the mixture on top of the blueberries, let it settle for a couple of minutes, then cook for 35–45 minutes, until the batter is golden and the blueberries' juice is bubbling up the sides of the cake tin.

> Remove the tin from the oven and run a palette knife around the edge to loosen the pudding. Leave to stand for a few minutes, then put a wire rack on top of the tin and flip it upside down to cool on the rack. This is nice served warm, with a big dollop of sour cream, plain yoghurt or crème fraîche, or kept in the fridge and eaten cool at any time of the day.

Maple glazed pear + hazelnut tart

I discovered this recipe while living in Vancouver, where fresh, locally grown hazelnuts were cheap, easy to come by and absolutely delicious, as were juicy pears from the Okanagan Valley. It's the kind of dessert that's great eaten warm, fresh from the oven with a big dollop of crème fraîche, but also lovely once it's been in the fridge for a day or so – I often used to find myself eating it for breakfast with some natural yoghurt. Either way, it's a comforting, moreish tart that really celebrates the harmony between sweet pears and crunchy hazelnuts.

½ batch of chilled sweet pastry (see page 207)

160 g (5½ oz) skinned, roasted hazelnuts, plus a few extra, halved, for garnish

½ teaspoon grated fresh ginger

110 g (3¾ oz/½ cup) golden caster (superfine) sugar

30 g (1 oz/¼ cup) plain (all-purpose) flour, plus extra for dusting

nutmeg, for grating

80 g (3 oz) unsalted butter, softened, plus extra for greasing

1 teaspoon vanilla extract

½ teaspoon almond extract

2 large eggs, at room temperature

2 firm pears

maple syrup, for glazing

SPECIAL EQUIPMENT

24 cm (10 in) pie dish

pastry brush

> Preheat the oven to 180°C (350°F/Gas 4) and grease the pie dish. Roll out the chilled pastry on a lightly floured work surface to 3 mm (⅛ in) thickness and about 2½ cm (1 in) wider than the pie dish. Using a floured rolling pin, carefully transfer it to the pie dish and drape it across the top. Let it sink into the dish, and, holding on to the edges, lift and tuck the pastry into the edges of the dish, all the way round, to line it. Trim off any excess pastry and lightly prick the base with a fork. Chill for 30 minutes.

> While the pastry is chilling, pulse the hazelnuts, the ginger and half the sugar in a food processor until finely ground, then add the flour and a good grating of nutmeg, and quickly pulse to combine.

> Using a hand-held electric mixer or stand mixer fitted with the paddle attachment, cream together the butter, remaining sugar and extracts until pale and fluffy. Add the eggs one at a time, beating thoroughly after each addition. Then gently stir through the nut mixture until it's totally incorporated.

> Remove the pastry from the fridge, line it with a piece of baking parchment and fill with baking beans. (Scrunch up the baking parchment before you line the dish and it will be more pliable and fit more snugly.)

> 'Blind' bake the pastry case for 10–15 minutes, until the edges are golden. Remove the parchment and baking beans, and bake for a further 3 minutes, until the pastry is set and the base is golden. Allow to cool for a few minutes, then spread the nut filling evenly into the tart shell. Halve and core the pears, then slice them lengthways, holding the slices together to retain their pear shape. Arrange 3 sliced pear halves on top of the filling, fanning the slices slightly and pressing them lightly into the filling. Scatter the halved hazelnuts around the pears, pressing them lightly into the filling. Bake for 30–40 minutes until the pears are golden and the frangipane is puffed and golden brown. When you remove it from the oven, use a pastry brush to brush the pears, but not the filling, with some maple syrup. Allow the tart to cool for about 15 minutes on a wire rack, slice and serve warm, or allow to cool completely and chill.

Serves

SERVES
6–8

Peanut butter ice cream

This peanut butter ice cream has become a little bit legendary among my friends and I think that's because I make my own peanut butter for the recipe. This is obviously one for the peanut butter fans out there, and it is very, very rich. I'd go as far as to say it's a little bit evil, in a good way.

PEANUT BUTTER

200 g (7 oz) roasted, unsalted peanuts

generous pinch of sea salt

2 tablespoons honey

100 ml (3½ fl oz) groundnut, peanut or walnut oil

CUSTARD

4 egg yolks

100 g (3½ oz/scant ½ cup) golden caster (superfine) sugar

300 ml (10 fl oz) double (heavy) cream

300 ml (10 fl oz) whole milk

½ teaspoon vanilla extract

1 quantity of peanut butter (see above)

40 g (1½ oz) roasted, unsalted peanuts, some whole, some roughly chopped

SPECIAL EQUIPMENT

ice cream maker

› To make the peanut butter, blitz the peanuts and salt in a food processor until they're finely chopped. Add the honey and oil, and blitz until you have a creamy peanut butter consistency. Taste, and add a touch more salt if required.

› To make the ice cream, in a large bowl whisk the egg yolks with half the sugar until frothy and pale. Put the cream, milk, vanilla extract, remaining sugar and peanut butter in a saucepan over a medium heat and stir until the mixture reaches boiling point. Remove from the heat and drop a teaspoon of the egg yolk and sugar mixture into the hot milk and cream and whisk it in to temper it. Then pour the hot milk and cream mixture in a steady stream into the egg mix, whisking continuously. Wash and dry the saucepan. Return the mixture to the pan and heat over a low-medium heat, for 3–4 minutes, until it is very hot but not boiling, and the mixture begins to thicken. It should coat the back of a wooden spoon or spatula, and leave a clear trail behind when you swipe your finger across it. Remove from the heat and leave to cool, then chill for 2 hours, or preferably overnight.

› Pour the custard into an ice cream maker and churn according to the manufacturer's instructions. Ten minutes before it's done, add the remaining peanuts. If not eating immediately, remove the paddle, transfer the ice cream to an airtight container or tray, cover and freeze.

› If you don't have an ice cream machine, you can still make this by pouring the mixture into a pre-chilled airtight container and freezing it for 2 hours, until the edges become icy and crystalised, then whisking thoroughly to break up any crystals, before freezing again until solidified.

DESSERTS + DRINKS

219

Lemon meringue posset

This super simple lemon meringue posset is a fabulous dessert to make ahead because once you've made the meringues and the possets all you need to do is assemble them and top them with a maraschino cherry. They look so pretty served in jam jars with the little meringue kisses adding a crunch to the smooth, rich, intense lemon cream.

POSSET

600 ml (20 fl oz) double (heavy) cream

140 g (5 oz/⅔ cup) caster (superfine) sugar

juice of 3 large, unwaxed lemons, grated zest of 2

maraschino cherries, to garnish

MERINGUE

2 medium egg whites, at room temperature

125 g (4 oz/generous ½ cup) caster (superfine) sugar

1 tablespoon ground almonds

1 tablespoon flaked almonds (optional)

SPECIAL EQUIPMENT

piping bag and star nozzle

➤ To make the posset, slowly heat the cream with the sugar in a saucepan, stirring, until it comes to the boil. Boil it for precisely 3 minutes and no more. Remove it from the heat and whisk in the lemon juice and zest. Divide the mixture between 6 clean glass jars, allow to cool, and transfer to the fridge to set for at least 3 hours, preferably overnight.

➤ Preheat the oven to 120°C (240°F/Gas ½) and line a greased baking sheet with baking parchment.

➤ Whisk the egg whites in the spotlessly clean bowl of a stand mixer, or using a hand-held electric mixer, until thick and fluffy and stiff peaks form. Gradually add the sugar, 1 tablespoon at a time, whisking constantly until it's thick and glossy and leaves clearly defined ribbons in the mixture when spooned.

➤ Fit the piping bag with a star nozzle and pipe tiny gems of meringue onto the baking sheet, leaving space around each one as they will puff up. Dust with ground almonds and, if you like, stick a few almond flakes carefully into a few of them. Bake in the oven for 1 hour 30 minutes, until crispy. When you turn the oven off, leave the meringues in the oven with the door closed to dry them out while the oven drops in temperature.

➤ Serve the possets with the meringues on top, dotted with maraschino cherries.

Raspberry + white chocolate jelly

T his recipe came to me at the start of summer, when raspberries were suddenly screaming to be bought from every local store, and I had a hankering for a good old-fashioned jelly with the gorgeous little fruits suspended inside. There's nothing better than raspberries and cream, so I decided to add a layer of white chocolate mousse for a bit of colour and textural contrast. This pretty jelly is dead easy to make – you just need to allow for setting time between layers, so you might want to make it the day before you want to serve it. These measurements are for my old glass jelly mould, but it's worth popping your mould on a scale, re-setting it to zero and then filling it with water to see how the volumes compare and adjusting the measurements accordingly.

For a 700 ml (24 fl oz) mould:

JELLY

vegetable oil, for greasing

5 sheets platinum grade leaf gelatine

300 ml (10 fl oz) pomegranate juice

50 ml (2 fl oz) fruity white wine, such as chardonnay

2 tablespoons caster (superfine) sugar

70 g (2½ oz) raspberries, crushed to a pulp, plus 8 whole raspberries

juice of ½ lemon

MOUSSE

2 sheets platinum grade leaf gelatine

100 ml (3½ fl oz) double (heavy) cream

80 g (3 oz) good-quality white chocolate

1 tablespoon caster (superfine) sugar

SPECIAL EQUIPMENT

jelly mould

pastry brush

➤ Grease the jelly mould, using a pastry brush to paint a little bit of oil over the entire inside of the mould, making sure you get into all the crevices and curves.

➤ For the jelly, first place the gelatine sheets in a bowl of ice-cold water and set to one side. Put the pomegranate juice, wine, sugar, 150 ml (5 fl oz) water and the pulped raspberries in a saucepan, and bring up to a gentle boil, until the sugar has dissolved. Taste and season with lemon juice to tone down the sweetness. Remove from the heat.

➤ Squeeze as much water as possible out of the gelatine sheets, then stir them into the warm berry liquid, whisking to dissolve them completely. Pour the mixture into the greased jelly mould, drop in the whole raspberries and leave to cool. Cover and chill for 3 hours, until set.

➤ To make the mousse, soak the gelatine sheets in a bowl of ice-cold water and set to one side. Whip the cream to soft peaks and put in the fridge.

➤ Melt the chocolate in a heat-proof bowl suspended over a pan of simmering water (a bain marie), making sure that the bowl doesn't touch the water, until completely melted. Remove from the heat.

➤ Heat 40 ml (1¼ fl oz) water in a pan and add the gelatine sheets (squeezed of excess water) and sugar. Bring to a simmer and heat until the gelatine and sugar have dissolved.

➤ Mix the gelatine mixture into the melted chocolate, stirring well to incorporate, and allow to cool slightly, but not so it starts to set. Fold this through the whipped cream with a whisk until it's smooth and shiny and mousse-like. Gently spoon the mousse over the jelly, cover the jelly mould with cling film (cling film), and leave to set in the fridge for 3 hours, or overnight.

➤ When you're ready to serve the jelly, fill a large bowl with warm water. Gently submerge the jelly mould, top down, and hold it in the water for 30 seconds. Use a very fine metal skewer to gently pierce the vacuum holding the jelly in the mould, by inserting it at the edge of the jelly. Place a serving plate over the open end of the mould, and, holding on to both the mould and the plate, flip it over so that the jelly is sitting on the plate. Lift off the mould, and serve.

I really LOVE the start of spring,

when here in England the trees are fragrant + floral with little white ELDERFLOWERS.* I've never lived anywhere where elderflower season has been so apparent, but I'm near the RIVER LEA + HACKNEY MARSHES, + when spring arrives, suddenly my morning runs + bike rides become heady with the GORGEOUS SCENT of these pretty + short-lived white flowers, which seem to grow from every tree. I love to fill bags + BAGS with them + preserve their fleeting flavour by making elderflower cordial, some of which I drink STRAIGHT AWAY with ice, fizzy water + lemon slices, + some of which I leave in the FRIDGE. When left for a few weeks, elderflower cordial ferments, +, like magic turns into naturally-alcoholic super-sweet FIZZ, which is perfect for using in SUMMER COCKTAILS.

Elderflower cordial/champagne

MAKES
**1.5 litres
(2½ pints)**

H*ere's my very simple cordial recipe. Whatever you do, don't be tempted to wash the elderflowers before you make it as that will wash away all the aromatic pollen which gives it its special scent and flavour.*

500 g (1 lb 2 oz/generous 2 cups) golden caster (superfine) sugar

zest of 2 unwaxed lemons, the lemons sliced into rounds

20 heads of elderflower

> Put the sugar into a large saucepan or casserole, cover with about 1.5 litres (52 fl oz) of water and heat until it's not quite boiling, but the sugar has dissolved. Remove from the heat and cool slightly, then add the sliced lemons, zest and elderflower heads. Stir and leave to steep for 24 hours.

> Sterilise a few jars and/or bottles by putting them through a hot dishwasher cycle or washing them in hot, soapy water, rinsing well and drying them in a hot oven for 10 minutes.

> Line a colander or sieve with a clean tea towel and place over a large bowl. Carefully pour the elderflower mixture into it, in stages if you need to, and allow it to filter through. Transfer to a jug and fill the sterilised bottles and/or jars with the cordial. It keeps for up to 6 weeks in the fridge, by which time it should have fermented into a lightly sparkling, very syrupy wine, ideal for the cocktail opposite.

Elderflower spritz

MAKES
1 cocktail

This is such a light, floral, summery cocktail. If you can't find elderflower cordial or haven't made your own, try replacing it with a bitter liqueur like Aperol or Campari, like they do in Italy, and omitting the gin. I like to make these in jam jars with plenty of ice and garnish them with gooseberries, elderflower or rose petals.

25 ml (1 fl oz) gin

25 ml (1 fl oz) elderflower champagne or cordial

75 ml (2½ fl oz) prosecco

soda water, to top up

TO GARNISH

fresh gooseberries

elderflowers

rose petals

> Pour the gin into the glass over ice with the elderflower champagne or cordial and add the prosecco. Top up with soda water and garnish with gooseberries and elderflowers. Cheers!

DESSERTS + DRINKS

227

CHAPTER 8

Essentials

THIS CHAPTER IS ALL ABOUT THOSE LITTLE EXTRAS THAT ADD A BIT OF 'WOW' TO YOUR COOKING ARSENAL.

I happen to believe that home-made preserves are one such extra. Yes, you can buy preserved lemons, but it's so much better to make them yourself (see page 233) as you can be clever about how you flavour them, and know exactly what you're putting in. In this chapter I show you how easy it is to make your own, and once you've got the hang of it, you'll find yourself wanting to share the spoils with everyone (and you'll have to stop yourself adding a little bit of preserved lemon to almost everything you cook). Sophie's pickled ceps (see page 234) have a similar addictive quality, and make a real difference to any salad or simple supper you might be throwing together. They are also very nice eaten on their own, like sweets.

The Cumin brioche (see page 245), an Indian-French fusion bread, came to me when I was trying to create a bread to accompany the spicy lamb Keema pau dish (see page 63), which begs for a light, fluffy bread to scoop it up. Cumin's fragrant warmth works wonderfully with the buttery brioche, and makes the perfect foil for fatty meats like lamb and bacon, which it sandwiches in the hangover- busting breakfast bap in the breakfast and brunch chapter.

My flavoured mayo recipes (see page 241) take everyday, store-bought mayonnaise and pimp it up into something altogether more interesting. I've also nabbed my pal Charlie's killer Dijon salad dressing recipe (see page 242), which I've coveted for years. Green salads will never be the same again...

ESSENTIALS

Preserved lemons

After simple preparation, all you need is a little bit of patience for the salt to work its magic before you can enjoy the brilliantly intense flavour of these preserved lemons. They are completely worth the wait! The first time I made them, I became obsessed with the salty, deep citrus edge they brought to my dishes, and worked through the jar in no time at all. While strongly associated with Middle Eastern cuisine and tagines, I find I use them for all sorts of things, from seasoning hot oil when frying off seafood, to making sauces for pasta dishes and salad dressings. I'd really encourage you to make a jar; it's a beautiful thing, and also makes a fantastic gift for friends.

130 g (4 oz) flaky sea salt

100 g (3½ oz/scant ½ cup) caster (superfine) sugar

1 sprig thyme, leaves picked

5 large unwaxed, organic lemons, scrubbed

1 tablespoon olive oil

SPECIAL EQUIPMENT

1 large preserving jar, approximately 800 ml (26 fl oz) capacity

> Sterilise the jar by putting it through a hot dishwasher cycle or washing it in hot, soapy water, rinsing well and drying it in a hot oven for 10 minutes.

> Mix the salt, sugar and thyme in a bowl. Slice the lemons very finely, removing and discarding the pips as you go. Have the sterilised jar ready, and scatter a pinch of the salt and sugar mixture on the bottom. Then take the lemon slices and dip one side in the salt and sugar mixture. Layer them, salty side down in the jar. Repeat the dipping and layering, occasionally scattering over some more of the salt and sugar mixture, and pressing the layers down to squeeze in the remaining lemon slices, until you've reached the top of the jar. By the end, the juice and brine should completely cover the lemon slices. Top with the olive oil, ensuring that none of the lemon is in contact with the air, and seal the jar. Store in the fridge for 2–3 months, waiting at least 1 week before opening it.

1 large jar

Sophie's pickled ceps

My friend Sophie Dening is a fantastic food and wine writer. We've spent a lot of time eating (and drinking) together, everywhere from cramped Soho sushi counters to Noma in Copenhagen, but wherever we are in the world, one thing's for sure – if there's a pickle on the menu, Sophie will order it. This is her favourite recipe for pickled dried ceps, and I think it's ingenious. It's dead simple, and really only calls for store-cupboard ingredients and a thumb of ginger, but the result is absolutely delicious and incredibly addictive. I can eat these straight from the jar, but they're very good in salads, with cold beef, on poached eggs or in sandwiches. Sophie says: 'This is a rock 'n' roll kinda recipe, except for one thing: it came about because of a spot of car trouble during a trip to the garden centre one day. Waiting for a lift home, I took refuge next door at Adam Coghlan's house. Adam is a would-be flâneur (his words), journalist, and leading light of London Restaurant Festival. That day, he pressed a bag of dried shiitake mushrooms into my hands and tipped me the wink. I duly went home and looked up a certain pickled shiitake recipe in the Momofuku cookbook. Ever since, these amazing 'shrooms have been like sweeties in my house. The idea of trying it with ceps came from my friend James Lowe.'

---

100 g (3½ oz) dried ceps

150 ml (5 fl oz) light soy sauce

150 ml (5 fl oz) cider vinegar

150 g (5oz/⅔ cup) golden caster (superfine) sugar

2 thumb-sized pieces of fresh ginger, peeled

SPECIAL EQUIPMENT

500 ml (17 fl oz) jar

> Sterilise the jar by putting it through a hot dishwasher cycle or washing it in hot, soapy water, rinsing well and drying it in a hot oven for 10 minutes.

> Place the ceps in a heatproof bowl and cover with boiling water. Leave to rehydrate for 15 minutes, then lift out with a slotted spoon. Reserve 200 ml (7 fl oz) of the mushroom liquid, passing it through a fine mesh sieve, and put it into a heavy-based saucepan with the soy sauce, vinegar, sugar, ginger and ceps. Simmer over a low heat for 30 minutes, then allow to cool. Discard the ginger, and pack the mushrooms into the sterilised jar, completely covering them with pickling liquid. Seal with vinegar-proof lids and store in the fridge for up to 1 month.

Chicken stock (+ poached chicken breast)

I can't recommend getting into the habit of making your own chicken stock enough. It's just so versatile: you can freeze it to use in sauces, risottos, stews or soups, or keep a jug of it in the fridge in the winter months ready to make impromptu broths with glass noodles, grated ginger, spring onion (scallion), chilli and poached chicken. It can be a real game-changer to have good stock in the fridge for making speedy, warming, immune-system boosting soup or stew. Use this recipe as a base and add aromatics of your choice to customise it; I like experimenting with Asian flavours like star anise, ginger and lemongrass. I use a whole bird to make my stock, which might seem a bit lavish, but it's something favoured by two of my food heroes, Uyen Luu and Alice Waters, and it really makes for a flavour- and goodness-packed stock. Plus, you end up with fantastic poached chicken, to shred into salads, pies or serve with rice or veg. Use the best chicken you can find – I find that corn-fed ones have more flavour.

1 x 1–1.5 kg (2 lb 3 oz–3 lb 2 oz) free-range, organic corn-fed chicken

5 black peppercorns

1 white onion, halved

2 garlic cloves

1 stick celery

1 carrot, peeled

1 star anise (optional)

1 bouquet garni of parsley stems, thyme and a bay leaf, tied together with kitchen-string

pinch of sea salt

fish sauce, to taste (optional)

➤ Place the chicken and all the remaining ingredients into a large saucepan or stockpot. Cover with about 4 litres (7 pints) cold water (the more you use the less intense the stock will be). Place over a medium heat and bring to a rolling boil, skimming off any scum or froth from the surface. As soon as it reaches a rolling boil immediately turn the heat down to a very gentle simmer, with small bubbles popping on the surface at irregular intervals. Do not allow it to boil for long as this will emulsify the fat, making a murky, greasy stock. Leave for up to 3 hours. The longer you leave it the more intense the stock will be. If it's reducing too rapidly, just add more water. After 1 hour remove the breasts and 'oysters' from the chicken and use them for salads or noodle soups, returning the carcass to the stock pan for the remaining time. Strain the stock through a fine mesh sieve, and, if you want a really fine clear stock, use a chemex filter or other pour-over coffee filter to strain it again. If you're using the stock straight away, season it with salt or fish sauce, to taste, and skim off any fat. If you're making it to use at a later date, pour it into a clean jug and leave the fat as it will act as a natural seal, and once chilled it will solidify so that it can be easily removed. Once completely cool, the stock will keep in the fridge for 1 week, or in the freezer for 2 months.

Hot health broth

Whenever I start to feel like I might be coming down with something, I bust out this quick, easy noodle soup and it's always a comfort. It reminds me of the Vietnamese noodle soup pho and is packed full of nutrients and health-giving ingredients like ginger, chilli and garlic. It's incredibly versatile because you can add whatever veg you might have lying around, adding fresh herbs, vegetables, bean sprouts and noodles of your choice. This is also a satisfying and light dish if you're trying to be good, or doing a fast diet, as it has hardly any calories (depending on what you put in it).

BASE

800 ml (28 fl oz) chicken stock (see opposite), or 600 ml (20 fl oz) stock and 200 ml (7 fl oz) water

1 teaspoon brown sugar

thumb-sized piece of fresh ginger, grated

2 spring onions (scallions), finely sliced

1 garlic clove, finely sliced

chestnut or shiitake mushrooms, sliced

½ bird's-eye chilli, finely sliced

1 carrot, grated

2 teaspoons fish sauce

lime, to garnish

OPTIONAL EXTRAS

handful of bean sprouts

poached or roasted shredded chicken

fresh coriander (cilantro) leaves

fresh mint leaves

1–2 teaspoons of freshly squeezed lime juice, to taste

udon or rice vermicelli noodles, blanched in hot water

kale, stems removed and leaves chopped

freshly ground black pepper

> Put all the base ingredients, except the fish sauce and lime, in a saucepan and simmer gently for 5 minutes. Season with fish sauce and lime juice, and pour into deep bowls. If you wanted to make this with noodles and chicken, pour it over some blanched rice vermicelli or udon noodles and shredded chicken at this stage. Garnish with fresh herbs, bean sprouts and a squeeze of lime. Season with black pepper.

Fish stock

Next time you go to the fishmonger, ask them for some fish heads and bones to make stock. If they're worth their salt, they'll happily wrap you up some of their offcuts (which would probably otherwise go in the bin). Fish stock is quick and easy to make, can be stored in the fridge or frozen in ice-cube bags and popped out to add a real depth of flavour to fish sauces and soups.

600 g (1 lb 5 oz) fish offcuts – heads and bones (eyes and gills removed)

80 ml (2½ fl oz) white wine, or leftover sparkling wine (that hasn't gone vinegary)

small bunch of parsley stalks, tied together

½ white part of a leek, sliced

1 stick celery, sliced

½ teaspoon fennel seeds

3 black peppercorns

3 teaspoons good-quality fish sauce

› Wash the fish bones and heads under cold running water for a couple of minutes to remove any blood (which would make the stock bitter). Put all the ingredients except the fish sauce in a large saucepan or stockpot and cover with 800 ml (28 fl oz) water. Place over a medium heat and bring to a gentle boil, skimming off any scum as you go. Reduce the heat and simmer the stock for 25–30 minutes. Remove from the heat and leave to stand for a further 20 minutes to allow the impurities to settle. Strain the stock through a fine mesh sieve, and if you want a really fine clear stock, use a chemex filter or other pour-over cofee filter to strain it again. Season with the fish sauce. Once completely cool, the stock will keep in the fridge for a few days, or in the freezer for up to 3 months.

Sriracha mayo

I don't bother making my own mayonnaise here because all subtlety goes out the window as soon as you add the Sriracha, or hot chilli sauce. This is so easy to make and you can customise it to your taste, so if you like more of a chilli kick, simply add more Sriracha. A word of warning: once you have a jar of this in your fridge you just might find yourself using it on everything – from a cheese sandwich to your Sunday roast.

2 tablespoons Sriracha
or similar chilli sauce

10 tablespoons good-quality
mayonnaise (I like Hellmann's)

grated zest and juice of ½ lime

pinch of sea salt

pinch of ground white pepper

> Sterilise a small jar by putting it through a hot dishwasher cycle or washing it in hot, soapy water, rinsing well and drying it in a hot oven for 10 minutes.

> Simply combine all the ingredients, season to your liking and store in the sterilised jar or a squeezy plastic bottle in the fridge.

Smoked paprika mayo

This little mayo recipe is the perfect foil for fish and seafood. It's great as a dip for peeled, prawns, grilled squid or drizzled over the Octopus carpaccio on page 70.

10 tablespoons good-quality
mayonnaise

3 tablespoons extra-virgin olive oil

6 teaspoons hot smoked paprika

3 teaspoons cayenne pepper

2 teaspoons garlic granules

1 tablespoon freshly squeezed
lemon juice

> Sterilise a small jar by putting it through a hot dishwasher cycle or washing it in hot, soapy water, rinsing well and drying it in a hot oven for 10 minutes.

> Mix all the ingredients together vigorously until you have a mayonnaise that you can easily drizzle and store in the sterilised jar or a squeezy plastic bottle in the fridge.

ESSENTIALS

241

Charlie's ultimate Dijon dressing

My friend Charlie is an excellent cook, and also a brilliant hostess. I've spent many a night at various stages of my life sitting around her dining table among friends, eating big portions of her perfect lasagne or famous cauliflower curry, washed down with a lot of wine. Like her mum Jane, whose home cooking used to line our stomachs before teenage nights out, she's a feeder, and I've always admired her way with a simple green salad. Her trick is this killer Dijon mustard-based dressing, which cloaks fresh crunchy leaves in a thick, velvety, perfectly-balanced vinaigrette. It's the only salad dressing you'll ever need. Charlie says: 'I love this dressing. It took me years to get it right, and tastes just like the one I had with an omelette and green salad when I was little in a simple French restaurant in the Alps. It's very, very straightforward. The trick is to not over-complicate it by adding lots of other things like herbs and garlic. The main thing is to use plenty of olive oil and heaps of Dijon. I like it with lettuce leaves and nothing else.'

---

pinch of sea salt

1 teaspoon sugar or
honey, to sweeten

1 tablespoon white wine vinegar

3 tablespoons Dijon mustard

4 tablespoons extra-virgin olive oil

> To make the dressing, dissolve the salt and sugar or honey in the vinegar. Add the mustard and olive oil and whisk until emulsified.

Chipotle salsa

This versatile salsa is given fiery, smoky depth by the chipotle chillies. I love slathering it onto fried eggs, eaten with my Guacamole bread (see page 36), and it's also great in a roast chicken sandwich. You can find chipotle chillies at specialist Mexican grocers or online, or you could replace with any chilli you can get hold of.

---

2 dried chipotle chillies

pinch of salt

½ white onion, cut in half

3 ripe tomatoes, halved

2 fat garlic cloves,
bashed but left whole

squeeze of lime juice

olive oil

> Place the dried chillies in a heatproof bowl and add about 300 ml (10 fl oz) boiling water. Leave for about 10 minutes to rehydrate, until soft all the way through. Place a griddle pan over a medium-high heat until really hot, dust with salt and then place the onion, tomatoes and garlic on it.

> Cook, turning occasionally, until the tomatoes and onion are soft (you might need to remove the garlic a bit earlier to avoid it burning) and the tomato skins are blackening.

> Drain the chipotles, reserving about 2 tablespoons of their rehydration liquid, and put them into a blender or food processor, along with the other ingredients, and blend until you have a smooth salsa. Add a splash of olive oil and blend once more. The salsa will keep for up to 4 days in the fridge in an airtight container.

Home-cooked crab meat

MAKES
1 dressed
crab

Picked crab meat is quite accessible in shops and fish mongers these days, as are dressed crabs, but nothing tastes quite as good as fresh crab meat you've cooked and picked yourself. It takes some patience to break down the crab and mine out all that gorgeous sweet flesh, but it's easy to do, quite a lot of fun, and well worth the hard work.

1 live crab (1 kg / 2 lb 3 oz)

½ bulb of fennel

4 black peppercorns

50 ml (2 fl oz) white wine
or white wine vinegar

½ lemon

½ white onion

1 bay leaf

sea salt

❯ Place all the ingredients apart from the live crab in a high-sided cooking pot or Le Creuset and bring to a rolling boil. Drop the crab into the water, and bring it back to the boil, cooking for 10–15 minutes, depending on the size (12 minutes per kilo is a good guide) and then remove from the liquid (bouillon) with a slotted spoon and leave to cool.

❯ Prepare 2 bowls for shells and meat, and a hand bowl of warm water to clean your hands as they'll get messy. Snap the legs and claws off from the main body and bash them with the back of a heavy knife (or a small hammer) to break the shell. Remove the claw and leg meat (you can use the end of a teaspoon as a pick), being sure to discard any of the hard membrane from the claw and feel carefully for bits of shell.

❯ Give the main body shell a good wipe with a clean cloth to get rid of any dirt. To separate the 'purse' – the part of the crab that the legs were attached to – from the outer shell, just put the crab on its back and push up on the purse. It should come away quite easily. Remove and discard the 'dead man's fingers' (the feathery gills attached to the purse or shell).

❯ Use a paring knife to score around the inner shell (follow the natural curved line on the overarching edges of shell), and remove it. Push the jaw down into the shell until it breaks away and remove it – the stomach sack will come away too. Scrape out the brown meat from the crab into a bowl, feeling through it to check for any shell. To get the meat from the purse, scrape all the meat from the top of it, cut it open and scrape the meat from inside it. I like to mix the white and brown meats together because I like the blend of strong nutty brown meat and sweet white meat, but you could keep them separate.

ESSENTIALS

Cumin brioche

These light demi-brioche buns, spiked with warm and earthy cumin, use less butter than standard brioche recipes, making them really soft and bouncy; ideal for toasting, buttering while hot and using to scoop up the gorgeous Keema pau *on page 63. They're also great for the Hangover-busting breakfast baps on page 44.*

240 ml (8 fl oz)
lukewarm water

40 ml (1¼ fl oz)
lukewarm whole milk

30 g (1 oz/scant ¼ cup)
caster (superfine) sugar

10 g (½ oz) dried
active yeast

470 g (1 lb 1 oz/3¾ cups)
plain (all-purpose) flour,
plus extra for dusting

1½ teaspoons salt

60 g (2 oz) chilled
unsalted butter, cubed

1 egg, beaten, plus
2 eggs for egg wash

1 tablespoon
ground cumin

oil, for greasing

1 tablespoon cumin seeds

sea salt, for sprinkling

SPECIAL
EQUIPMENT

stand mixer

pastry brush

> Combine the warm water, milk, sugar and yeast in a bowl, stir well and leave for a few minutes until it's puffing and bubbling.

> Put the flour, salt and butter into a separate mixing bowl, and rub in the butter until the mixture is the consistency of breadcrumbs. For ease, you could use a stand mixer fitted with the paddle attachment to do this. Stir in the beaten egg, ground cumin and the yeast mix, mixing it on a low setting if using a stand mixer, for a few minutes until you have a sticky, scruffy dough. If mixing by hand, just stir with a wooden spoon until well-combined, turn out onto a heavily floured surface, flour your hands and rub them together, and work the mix for 5–7 minutes, until the dough comes together. It will be very wet and sticky at first but don't worry – this makes for a light dough.

> Shape the dough into a ball and return it to the mixing bowl, greased with a little butter or oil. Cover the bowl with a damp tea towel and put in a warm place (I like to find a sunny windowsill) to rest for 1–3 hours until the dough has doubled in size.

> Turn the dough out onto a floured surface and punch the dough to knock out any air. Using a sharp knife or dough scraper, divide the dough into 8 equal portions (you can weigh each one on baking paper to make sure they're equal if you like). Flatten out each portion, and fold the edges into the middle, pinching gently in the middle to make a circular shape. Gently flip them over so they're seam side down and, one at a time, hardly touching them, clasp your hand over each portion, with your fingers encasing them and touching the work surface, and move your hand round and round (as though you're drawing clockwise circles), to create a nice round shape.

> Transfer the buns to a baking sheet lined with baking parchment, cover with oiled cling film (plastic wrap) and rest for 1 hour, or until they've risen again by about a third and puffed up. During the prove the buns may bond together, but don't be alarmed as you can break them apart once baked.

> Preheat the oven to 200°C (400°F/Gas 6). Half-fill a baking tin with boiling water and place it in the bottom of the oven – this will create steam to help crisp the top of the brioche. Whisk the remaining eggs with a splash of water, and gently brush each bun with egg wash. Scatter over the cumin seeds and some flakes of sea salt, and bake for 15–20 minutes, until crisp on top and golden brown. Remove from the oven and transfer to a wire rack to cool.

Making your own
CHICKEN + FISH stock
is a *game-changer.*

Thank yous

T hank you to my wonderful blog and Twitter followers for your ongoing support and enouragment. You guys are the reason I ever even dreamed about writing *A Lot On Her Plate*. You guys rule!

Writing this book has really been one of the single most exciting, creative and challenging projects I have ever embarked on, and I couldn't have done it without the support and understanding of my nearest and dearest. Jamie, thank you for being the most amazingly supportive, kind, considerate, funny and greedy man I know, for being a perpetual sounding board, always trying my creations with an open mind and telling me candidly what you think. I couldn't have done this without you (you super taster, you) and I love you a ridiculous amount.

There are so many people I need to thank for their help and encouragement, starting with my two key collaborators: my amazing publisher Kate, who took a gamble on this maverick (I love saying that), and my phenomenally talented photographer Helen Cathcart. Kate, working with you has been such a joy, you've always 'got' what I am trying to do with this book, and have given me an incredible amount of creative freedom and invaluable guidance, while always looking like an absurdly glamorous film star from the future. Thank you.

Helen, you've been with me every step of the way, thank you for always believing in me and for helping me to even dream that I might be able to do this. This all started with us playing around with some recipes in my old flat in Brixton, after a chance meeting (thanks to Dave Drummond for introducing us) where we bonded over burgers. I feel so super lucky to have worked with such a gifted food photographer, your pictures are amazing, you are a genius, and above all a dear, dear friend. This book would not be what it is without you! Here's to the dream team.

Massive thanks to the brilliant crew at Hardie Grant who have made this process as smooth as it possibly could be – the gorgeous Kajal Mistry, Emma Marijewycz and Stephen King. Thank you also to the super-talented Julia Murray for your stunning design – you've done a beautiful job.

I have been so lucky to have had a whole eager crew of fantastic recipe testers who have been so generous with their time and feedback. Pete and Maggie (Mr and Mrs Barker – whoop!), you have gone above and beyond and been so absolutely brilliant, you are the greatest friends I could hope for, thanks so much for all your testing and support, and Maggie for assisting during the shoot. Stephanie Boote: having you help on the shoot was superb, you are a great chef and an amazing pal, thanks for all the laughs and bay leaf jokes! Ben Blackburn, thank you for all your thorough and knowledgeable recipe testing, and for quoting Alan Partridge to me when I met you. Thanks to the lovely Jenny Brown for your help on the shoot too. Go team!

Thanks to Kate and Andrew Dolleymore for allowing me to neglect my gorgeous godson Leo while writing this, and for your general aceness and recipe testing. Thanks to Louise Bell for all your fab testing and to all my other top-notch testers – Georgia Bateman, Jessica Wong, Anne-Marie Booth, Kate McAuley. A big thank you to Fiona Hemming and Cuisinart, to Grace and Thom Flowers, and to Kitchenaid.

Thanks so much to my sister Alice and bro-in-law Simon for their ongoing support, for letting me be an absent aunty to the adorable Otis and for being general stars. To my soul sister, Uyen Luu, who has been a great friend, mentor and huge inspiration – you are a superstar and you know you played a big part in all this. Thanks to Gizzi Erskine for her inspiration, kindness and support.

To my London-by-way-of-Maidstone family for all the love, laughter and plotting over copious food and drink – Charlotte Wharfe (who also supplied the brilliant Dijon dressing recipe), Liz Marvin and Annie Bashford.

Thanks to all those who contributed some wonderful recipes – Sophie Dening, James Lowe, Naved Nasir, Vivek Singh, Elly Curshen. Thanks to Chris Galvin (who supplied the lovely foreword) and Andy Lynes for being ongoing career mentors and good friends.

Big thank yous to my wonderful editors Chris Hayes, Lulu Grimes and Mina Holland: your support while writing this has been so precious and you've been so generous with your advice and knowledge. Thanks to Dom Dwight and Dan Jeffrey for giving me my first break – I wouldn't be here now if it weren't for you. Talk a full moon kitchen!

And finally, thanks Mum and Dad for starting this whole thing. I love you dearly and the food, love and support you gave me growing up is the reason I am writing this now.

ABOUT THE AUTHOR

Rosie Birkett is a food writer, food stylist + home cook. She writes for magazines such as OLIVE, GRAZIA + JAMIE OLIVER Magazine + newspapers including THE GUARDIAN + THE INDEPENDENT. Her food styling has appeared in the Guardian's food supplement COOK + in OLIVE magazine, as well as on her popular blog from which this book takes its name.

As an authoritative food writer + editor she has worked with some of the **world's best chefs,** built up a significant following on TWITTER + appeared on MASTERCHEF + LONDON LIVE. In 2013, after writing a foodie guidebook with the world-renowned chef **Alain Ducasse** called J'AIME LONDON, she spent 4 months living in VANCOUVER, BRITISH COLUMBIA, + writing, cooking + travelling throughout the STATES + MEXICO.

She lives in HACKNEY, EAST LONDON.

A Lot on Her Plate by Rosie Birkett

First published in 2015 by Hardie Grant Books

Hardie Grant Books (UK)
Dudley House, North Suite
34–35 Southampton Street
London WC2E 7HF
www.hardiegrant.co.uk

Hardie Grant Books (Australia)
Ground Floor, Building 1
658 Church Street
Melbourne, VIC 3121
www.hardiegrant.com.au

British Library Cataloguing-in-Publication Data. A catalogue record
for this book is available from the British Library.

ISBN: 978-174270-914-7

Publisher: Kate Pollard
Senior Editor: Kajal Mistry
Cover, Internal Design and Illustrations: Julia Murray
Photography: © Helen Cathcart
Copy Editor: Laura Nickoll
Proofreaders: Susan Pegg and Simon Davis
Indexer: Cathy Heath
Colour Reproduction by p2d

Printed and bound in China by 1010

Find this book on **Cooked.**
Cooked.com.au
Cooked.com

10 9 8 7 6 5 4 3 2 1